Peter Markl
Erich Kadlec
(eds.)

Karl Popper's Response to 1938

PETER LANG
Frankfurt am Main · Berlin · Bern · Bruxelles · New York · Oxford · Wien

Bibliographic Information published by the Deutsche Nationalbibliothek
The Deutsche Nationalbibliothek lists this publication in the Deutsche Nationalbibliografie; detailed bibliographic data is available in the internet at <http://www.d-nb.de>.

Cover picture: Karl Popper.
By kind permission of the Estate of Sir Karl Popper.

Logo: Karl Popper Institute.
By permission of the Karl Popper Institute.

With support of the Federal Ministry for European and International Affairs of Austria.

ISBN 978-3-631-58134-6
© Peter Lang GmbH
Internationaler Verlag der Wissenschaften
Frankfurt am Main 2008
All rights reserved.

All parts of this publication are protected by copyright. Any utilisation outside the strict limits of the copyright law, without the permission of the publisher, is forbidden and liable to prosecution. This applies in particular to reproductions, translations, microfilming, and storage and processing in electronic retrieval systems.

Printed in Germany 1 2 3 4 5   7

www.peterlang.de

Contents

1 Introduction: Remembering 1938 7

2 Bryan Magee: Placing Popper 13

3 Troels Eggers Hansen: Popper's Early Work on the Theory of Knowledge 29

4 Hubert Kiesewetter: The Birth of Karl Popper's The Open Society and Its Enemies 45

5 Erich Kadlec: Popper's "Negative Utilitarianism" – From Utopia to Reality 107

6 Peter Markl: "Popper's Path from Evolutionary Biology to his late Evolutionary Thinking" 123

7 Gerhard Budin: Popper's Theory of Objective Knowledge and Its Relevance in Modern Knowledge Society 149

Contributors 161

Remembering 1938

Seventy years ago, on March 12th 1938, Hitler's troops crossed the Austrian border starting the occupation of Austria. This open military aggression was a violation of international law and made Austrian the first of a number states who became victims of Hitler's aggressive use of military power to achieve his aims. Years ago Hitler had already announced his plans for an annexation of Austria. After five years of futile attempts to destabilize the country by terrorist attacks on Austrian territory and extreme political pressure from outside, the Austrian government announced a plebiscite on Austrian independence planed for March 13, 1938. When the Austrian government insisted on holding the plebiscite Hitler increased the political pressure by new demands. Having reached to limit of political concessions the Austrian government gave way to political force on the evening of March 11. But fearing a negative outcome of the plebiscite Hitler had already decided for the military invasion of Austria. On March 15th, 1938, Hitler, from the balcony of the Imperial Palace in Vienna, could report "to history" the annexation of Austria into the German Reich. Austria had vanished from the map.

The international reaction to this blatant violation of international law was extremely sobering and disappointing. Austria had been a sovereign member state of the League of Nations and signatory of the Briand-Kellogg Peace Pact. Austria had, however, ceased to be a parliamentary democracy in 1933 and was deeply split by a bloody civil war in 1934. From the point of view of other democratic governments these facts did not strengthen arguments for another open confrontation with Hitler. The Austrian government was left alone and the population exposed to a machinery of terror actively established, supported and executed with the participation of Austrian National Socialists.

When Karl Popper received the news on the events in March 1938 in Vienna, he was shocked, but hardly surprised. He had expected this turn of event. Later, in his Autobiography, he wrote: "I expected, from 1929 on, the rise of Hitler; I expected the annexation of Austria by Hitler, in some form or other; and I expected the war against the west".

He had emigrated to New Zealand in 1937 where he found his first academic position as Senior lecturer in philosophy at Canterbury University College in Christchurch. He had left family members, colleagues and friend in Vienna: sixteen members of his family – cousins, uncles, aunts – did not survive the terror of the Nazis. Popper organized a Refugee Emergency Committee which had some limited success – by early 1939 the Committee had succeeded in achieving 31 Refugee permits for New Zealand. After the outbreak of World War II Popper tried to join the New Zealand Army as a volunteer, but was rejected. He continued work on subjects he had already started in Vienna but under the impression of March 1938 decided to postpone (almost) all other work and to elaborate his political philosophy.

Popper worked against the background of an increasingly darkening horizon: in September 1938, as a result of the Munich agreement, Hitler took over the German speaking regions of the so-called Sudetenland and in March 1939 occupied the remaining territory of Czechoslovakia before launching World War II in September 1939 with the invasion of Poland. In retrospect Popper also mentioned the Hitler-Stalin Pact of August 1939 as contributing to the feeling of urgency which has never left him while working on this task. Whenever his teaching load – he was the only one teaching philosophy in Canterbury – allowed it, he worked around the clock to the point of exhaustion at what he regarded as his "war effort".

The result achieved in the years from 1938 to 1943 were manuscripts which – after a rather complicated publication history – ended in form of two books which became classics in political philosophy:

THE POVERTY OF HISTORICISM

THE OPEN SOCIETY AND ITS ENEMIES.
VOL. 1: THE SPELL OF PLATO"
VOL. 2: THE HIGH TIDE OF PROPHECY: HEGEL, MARX, AND THE AFTER-MATH"

Popper regarded both books as "more or less complementary". He based his work on the methodology of science published in 1934 in his "Logik der Forschung" and on a manuscript he had drafted in summer 1935 which already carried the heading "The Poverty of Historicism". This first draft was developed into two lectures he held in Brussels and London in January 1936. Initially he focussed on "historicism" – the idea that there are general laws which describe the inevitable course of history forming the only "scientific" bases for historical prediction.

Dictators like Hitler or Stalin – and many before and after them – pretended to act in accordance with inevitable historical necessities which they somehow knew since they knew the laws of history. In spite of all their ideological differences Hitler and Stalin were united in their belief in inevitable laws of history although they had quite different ideas on the character of these laws and how they had obtained this knowledge. Many historicists claim to know how societies inevitably change in time, since they know the laws governing these changes – Marxists even regarded these laws as "scientific" laws, somehow analogous to the laws which allow the prediction of changes in physical systems or the "laws" of biological evolution. Others denied that physics or biology can serve as a model for such laws and resort to – for instance – an intuitive knowledge of the developmental laws of more or less holistic systems like societies.

Popper, however, showed, that in spite of their plausibility, both claims are "gross misunderstandings of the methods of science". These misunderstandings lead to a catastrophic neglect of the distinction between scientific prediction and historical prophecy. Not knowing this essential distinction or becoming victims of deliberate attempts to blur it in order to sell historical prophecies as scientific predictions has cost the life of many millions of people. In his autobiography Popper pointed out that "The Open Society" had initially been sort of a by-product of his elaboration of ideas which had – in rudimentary form – already been contained in the draft of summer 1935. But "in the systematic analysis and criticism of the main claims of historicism", he also "collected some material to illustrate its development" – notes which later became incorporated in "The Open society"

Upon finalizing the first chapter of the "The Poverty of Historicism" Popper realised that this text would attain such dimensions as to require the extraction of the exploding new concept of an Open Society and the separation of the text in two books. He decided to restrict "The Poverty of Historicism" to the contents formerly envisaged and finished the first three chapters , while the last chapter was written after finishing the draft version of volume I of the Open Society. In his autobiography, Popper attributes this "somewhat confused" genesis to the inner development of his thoughts, but also to the Hitler-Stalin Pact and the outbreak of World War II. In trying to imagine possible post-war worlds he felt that arguments in defence of freedom, against totalitarian and authoritarian ideas, and against moral relativism – which holds that any set of values can be defended – gained special importance.

As Popper has pointed out, his analysis of historicism does not claim something like scientific status. And it does not try to discuss events and decisions in historical detail. But it tries to answer the question why so many people found and find historicist prophecies by false prophets so plausible. He traces the source of this acceptance down to its origins in Greek philosophy – to the ideas of Plato and their interpretation and to Hegel and Marx.

Popper's two books are an important contribution the philosophy of democracy which he does not idealize. The Open society is a polemic plea for an open democratic society, with institutions established to support rational criticism and the possibility to remove governments which refuse to learn from errors. A plea for a society where utopian planning is substituted by piecemeal engineering based on an ethics which gives priority to what has been called "Popper's Negative Utilitarianism": not to the vague and utopian "Maximize Happiness" but to the modest, realistic and morally more urgent appeal "Minimize Suffering", as far as possible.

In 1960 – after the defeat of fascist regimes – Popper devoted his "Poverty of Historicism"

TO THE MEMORY OF THE COUNTLESS MEN, WOMEN AND CHILDREN
OF ALL CREEDS OR NATIONS OR RACES
WHO FELL VICTIM TO THE NATIONALIST AND COMMUNIST BELIEF
IN INEXORABLE LAWS OF HISTORICAL DESTINY

The "Open Society" turned out to be a great success from the very beginning. It was published in many revised and enlarged editions and translated into 23 languages but it was unwelcome and even banned in many totalitarian systems. It was widely distributed in the underground in the form of smuggled books or as typewritten Samizdat versions. It stood for the hope for democracy as the only system to prevent tyranny and for the expectation that oppressive political systems with utopian planning against the interests of its citizen cannot continue for long. In spite of the fact that it pleaded for humanity and tolerance and change by critically controlled piecemeal engineering Poppers critical rationalism seemed to be the greatest danger for totalitarianism since it was combined with personal yearning for individual liberty.

In recalling the dark days of March 1938 the editors hope to arouse new interest in Popper's analysis of ideas which are the ideological basis of all authoritarian political tendencies, organisations and regimes. In their original form, or some disguise or other, these ideas are still around. Sir

Karl Popper's passionate plea for democracy, individual freedom and open societies is as important today as it was in 1938.

Peter Markl	Erich Kadlec

Placing Popper

Bryan Magee

It is almost inevitable, of course, that when a radical innovator of any kind comes on the scene, everyone else is still actively thinking in terms that do not accommodate him. They try to understand him in terms of the categories they have – they could scarcely do otherwise at first – and therefore, with equal inevitability, they misunderstand him. There is a situational logic to such misunderstandings. People naturally start by applying what they take to be the new ideas to their own chief concerns; but this is to proceed as if the newcomer were addressing himself to the same problems as they are – and, of course, as a radical innovator he may not be. So from the beginning he gets pigeon-holed in inappropriate ways; and it may be a long time before the way he is seen escapes from this, and he starts being looked at in his own terms. Another form of misrepresentation that naturally occurs is that some of the first criticisms directed at the newcomer, because they rest on misunderstandings of what it is he is saying, do not actually apply to him; yet they may come to be widely accepted by people who themselves share the false assumptions involved, and may go on being repeated for a very long time.

All these things happened to Karl Popper, not just at this point or that in his philosophy but on a large scale. And we are still sufficiently close to him in time for them still to be obscuring the view of him that prevails in many quarters.

The misunderstandings began in Vienna in the 1920s. Vienna was Popper's home town, and in some very deep psycho-emotional way the Vienna of his youth remained "home" to him for the rest of his life. It was the soil in which he felt himself to be rooted; and this feeling was fully compatible with a powerful love of his adopted country, Great Britain, in which he chose to remain. In Popper's first decade of adult life, the 1920s, some of the most exciting and lastingly important developments in philosophy to be occurring anywhere in the world were happening in the University of Vienna. A group still referred to as the Vienna Circle released into the world a breed of philosophy known as Logical Positivism. Most of the main figures of this movement had been trained not as philosophers but as scientists or mathematicians, and what they were really trying to do was to formulate their scientific worldview in philosophical terms; indeed, to the manifesto they published they gave the title "The Scientific View of the World". They regarded the idealist metaphysics that had been so influential in the German-speaking world in which they had grown up as a lot of high-flown nonsense, pernicious in its effects on human thinking. And like many scientists of that era they had no time for religion. So one of their chief concerns was to eliminate any influence of metaphysics or religion from serious thought. To this end they came up with the famous Verification Principle, which is what they have ever since been best known for. This was a criterion of meaning, and held that to be genuinely meaningful a statement must belong to one of two logical kinds. Either its truth or falsehood must be ascertainable from a careful analysis of the statement itself, without reference to empirical facts – examples would be statements in logic or mathematics – or its truth or falsehood must be ascertainable by reference to the facts.

All statements about the empirical world were required to meet the latter criterion. If the truth or falsehood of an apparently factual statement made no observable difference to anything then it had no real content, no meaning. It is not necessary that a statement about the world that is empirically verifiable turn out to be true: it might turn out to be false: but one that was not verifiable even in principle was meaningless, and therefore incapable of being either true or false, because it was vacuous, empty.

The young Popper pointed out to the Logical Positivists that their Verification Principle wiped out not only metaphysics and religion but the whole of natural science. This was because scientific laws are not capable of empirical verification. As David Hume pointed out more than two and a half centuries ago, from no number of empirical observation statements, however large, does an unrestrictedly universal statement logically follow. But a scientific law is an unrestrictedly general statement about the empirical world, so this means that no finite number of observation statements can ever entail it. This was Popper's principal, and utterly devastating, objection to Logical Positivism. But he had others too. He pointed out that before we could possibly know how to go about verifying an empirical statement we needed first to understand what it means, and therefore our knowing how to verify it cannot be the criterion of its meaningfulness. He pointed out also that if only analytic, i.e. tautological, statements and empirically verifiable statements (and their negations) have any meaning, then any debate about a criterion of meaning is bound to contain meaningless statements, because no such debate can be conducted only in terms of tautologies and empirically verifiable statements. A spectacular illustration of this is the Verification Principle itself: it is neither a tautology, nor is it empirically verifiable: so according to itself it is meaningless.

Popper's arguments, set out by him in 1934 in his first published book, Logik der Forschung, translated into English much later as the The Logic of Scientific Discovery, destroyed Logical Positivism with complete effectiveness at the level of argument, and when eventually Logical Positivism was abandoned it was primarily for these reasons. But at first, and for a long time, the Logical Positivists simply did not realize that their position had been destroyed, and this was because they misinterpreted Popper by understanding him in their own terms. Because they were trying to formulate a criterion of meaning they thought Popper was trying to do much the same thing. And because they were being made increasingly aware during the course of the debate of the snags attaching to verification as a criterion, they took this man Popper to be cunningly suggesting falsification instead.

But Popper was doing no such thing. He always believed that to spend much time arguing over the meanings of words was unfruitful and boring, and, what is worse, based on a logical mistake. The logical mistake is this. If we are challenged to define a term, we need to introduce at least one new term into our definition, otherwise the definition will be circular. But then we can with equal legitimacy be challenged to define the new term. So we find ourselves in an infinite regress. The principle that we cannot have a worthwhile discussion until we have first defined our terms has the direct logical consequence that we can never have a worthwhile discussion at all, because we can never complete the necessary preliminaries. To put the same point the other way round, all discussion, including all worthwhile discussion, has to make use of undefined terms: there is no alternative. In illustration of this, Popper pointed to the natural sciences. It is an undeniable fact that natural scientists tend to spend little or none of their time debating the meanings of the terms they most habitually use – physicists, for example, are not noted for their debates about the meanings of terms such as light, mass, energy, and so on, nor for their discussions of the meanings of terms in mathematics – and yet the natural sciences constitute far and away the biggest, and the most practically useful, and the fasted growing, body of knowledge that human beings possess. Manifestly it is not the case that defining our terms is a necessary precondition of gaining knowledge or understanding.

Incidentally, because he held these views, when Popper found himself living in post-Second-World-War Britain in the heyday there of linguistic analysis he found himself also in the same root-and-branch opposition to the prevailing fashion in philosophy as he had been in inter-war Vienna. All his life he was the odd man out. But let us return to the Logical Positivists. When Popper told them that he was proposing falsifiability not as a criterion of empirical meaningfulness but as a criterion of demarcation between science and non-science they replied that it came to the same thing anyway, because only statements which satisfied the logical requirements of science were empirically meaningful, and therefore a criterion of demarcation between science and non-science must also be, at the same time, a criterion of demarcation between sense and non-sense. But again, Popper did not agree with that either, so the Logical Positivists were once again misunderstanding him by taking for granted that he shared with them assumptions that he did not share. He gave yet more reasons for believing that not only empirically unverifiable statements, but also empirically unfalsifiable ones, were not necessarily meaningless, and some of these again concerned science itself. For example, the pre-scientific beliefs out of which the sciences historically emerged contained a great deal of myth, magic and religion; and Popper maintained that it was credible neither empirically nor logically that the meaningful hypotheses and propositions of science should have developed out of predecessor hypotheses and propositions that were meaningless.

The leading historian of the Vienna Circle, Victor Kraft, who was also one of its members, has made clear how, over a period of years, the Logical Positivists made one concession after another to Popper, and therefore came closer and closer to him on particular points, without ever grasping how radically exclusive of their position his was. To their credit, they published his criticisms of them in their journal Erkenntnis; and one member, Otto Neurath, nicknamed him "the Official Opposition". They saw him as an awkward customer on the same playing field as themselves who was kicking the same ball around but uncompromisingly going his own way and trying to get the rules changed, and therefore they saw him as a sort of dissident positivist – and therefore as a sort of positivist. This was how he came to be more widely seen at that time; and that view of him has persisted to this day in quite a number of quarters: new publications continue to come out in which Popper is referred to as a positivist. But the truth is that Popper, who never attended a single meeting of the Vienna Circle, was never, at any time in his life, a positivist of any kind. On the contrary, he was the decisive anti-positivist.

Another major field in which Popper's contribution came to be characterized by many people as the direct opposite of what it should have been is political philosophy. As a young man Popper was a passionate socialist.

And as one of his friends from that time expressed it to me, he lived his socialism: he lived among the unemployed and the poor, dressed as they did, worked with handicapped children, got himself apprenticed to a skilled manual trade, even at one time tried to do unskilled manual labour. Like a great many such people, he moved to the right in middle age; but it is beyond dispute that from his teens until he was on the threshold of middle age he was a democratic socialist. And it was during these years that he worked out the political philosophy expressed in a book that he wrote very largely in his late thirties, The Open Society and Its Enemies. In my opinion, The Open Society constitutes the most powerful and plausible philosophy of democratic socialism that anyone has ever formulated. Because of the Second World War it was written in English, in New Zealand, and published for the first time in England. There it influenced two generations of Labour politicians, one of which included me; and some of its concepts have become standard terms of discourse in the British Labour Party, including the term "open society". But because Popper's philosophy was above all democratic it was passionately anti-totalitarian, and therefore both anti-Communist and anti-Marxist. The Open Society contains what many people regard as the most effective intellectual demolition of Marxism ever written. For this reason it was hated and feared by Marxists and their sympathizers all over the world, who denounced it as a reactionary book. In the post-Second-World-War world there were many countries whose intellectual classes were predominantly Marxisant – France, for instance, and Italy, and several countries in Latin America – so the denunciation of Popper as a right-wing reactionary was international. When he died in 1994, the leading left-wing Sunday newspaper in Britain, The Observer, gave the news the headline: "Hero of the Right Dies", and many other left-wing papers described him as a guru of free market economics. But the philosophy put forward in The Open Society is simply not that at all – you have only to read the book to see that. The briefest of quotations will put the matter beyond dispute. On page 125 of volume ii of The Open Society you will find the following two sentences. "If we wish freedom to be safeguarded, then we must demand that the policy of unlimited economic freedom be replaced by the planned economic intervention of the State. We must demand that unrestrained capitalism give way to economic interventionism." That's the spirit in which the whole book is written. But one thing the Communists were always brilliant at was propaganda, including the misinterpretation and smearing of their opponents. They never acknowledged even the existence of a democratic left, because they would never admit that they themselves were undemocratic.

They always represented anyone seriously opposed to them as being right-wing. There was one period in the fascinating history of their propaganda, in the 1930s, when they labelled all democratic socialists "social fascists". Anyone at any time who opposed them forcefully and effectively was likely to be labelled by them as fascist, or at the very least reactionary. And they were very clever at making mud stick. Of course, because Popper's criticism of Marxism was so large-scale and so devastating it was seized on with glee and made use of by conservatives – what else could one possibly expect? But that does not make the book in which it was done a right-wing book. It is true that after he had written the book, Popper – like, I suspect, most passionate young socialists – moved somewhat to the right, in his middle age. But I discussed politics with him frequently throughout the last 36 years of his life, and I can testify that at no time was we ever a devotee of unrestricted free-market economics. In any case, the political philosophy by which the world knew him then and knows him now is that of his book The Open Society and Its Enemies, and that is indisputably a book written by a young, or youngish, social democrat.

Now that Communism has been largely discredited it is time for people to look in a new light not only at Communists but also at their opponents. These were not, in most cases, as the Communists and their sympathizers painted them. Many people in the recent past were demonized by the left who were not only not demons but were on the left themselves. Another example is George Orwell. It is almost incredible now to remember that T.S. Eliot, whose own political and social views were indeed reactionary, refused in his capacity as director of a publishing house, Faber&Faber, to publish what are now Orwell's most famous novels, on the ground that they would give offence to the Soviet Union. But then Communists and conservatives always did have one very fundamental thing in common: they both detested liberalism. They both hated and feared the democratic left. When Khrushchev visited Britain he said that if he were an Englishman he would vote Conservative.

Popper's achievements as a thinker were both negative and positive. As a critic he was the supreme destroyer of the dominant myths of the twentieth century. At the century's beginning a certain view of science was held by almost everyone, scientist and non-scientist alike, namely that what distinguished science chiefly from other attempts to gain knowledge was its certainty: scientific knowledge was reliable, rock solid; and science consisted of an ever-growing body of such certainties. The two individuals who did more than any others to destroy this conception of science were

Einstein and Popper. Popper was also the most effective critic of Marxism, and in addition to that the first as well a the best critic of Logical Positivism. In the English-speaking world, throughout the whole of the period when linguistic-analytic philosophy reigned supreme, he was the most formidable of its opponents. The sum total of these intellectual achievements is immense, and would itself be enough to make Popper a figure of lasting importance in the history of ideas.

Even as a critic, though, he has been not infrequently misunderstood. The household gods of the young intellectuals in the Vienna in which Popper grew up were Marx and Freud, and he is often to this day described as having dismissed their ideas as complete rubbish. But he did no such thing. What he did was destroy their claims to be scientific – and that is something totally different. No one would dream of treating the myths of ancient Greece as if they were scientific theories, yet nearly everyone seems to agree that they are teeming with ideas and insights of great depth, penetration and value. Something like this was Popper's attitude to the works of Marx and Freud. He thought they were full of good ideas, and he paid high tribute to them for that. One of the concepts employed in the central argument of The Open Society and Its Enemies, "the strain of civilization", is adopted directly from Freud's marvellous little book Civilization and Its Discontents, and Popper acknowledges that in his own book. He also, in the same book, pays frequent tribute to the genius of Marx, and to the quality of some of his ideas and insights. Unfortunately, however, for both Marx and Freud, something that was absolutely central to their claims for what they themselves were doing was that they were putting their respective fields of thought on a scientific foundation for the first time. Marx had utter contempt for what he called "Utopian Socialism", and believed that the supreme value of what he was doing was that he was making socialism, for the first time, scientific: and he actually called his political philosophy "Scientific Socialism". Freud, similarly, believed that he was putting psychology on a solidly based scientific foundation for the first time, and that therein lay the chief and lasting value of what he was doing. It was these claims, in both cases, that Popper demolished, with what seems to be lasting effectiveness. And that, of course, is enough to explain why committed or even just enthusiastic followers of Marx and Freud reacted to Popper's work with such antagonism and dismay, depending on the degree of their understanding of it. They saw this man Popper as trying to take away from their idol, whether Marxism or psychoanalysis, its most important attribute, what gave it its unique power. And the fact that he muttered compliments to it while doing so seemed to them pro forma and irrelevant, and probably insincere in any case. But in truth the fact remains that Popper regarded both Marx and Freud as thinkers of exceptional originality and power, and thought of himself has having learnt valuable things from them – and always said so, in his book as well as in his conversation.

Even at Popper's level, it is easier to criticize the ideas of others than to put forward ideas of one's own. But Popper always did put forward ideas of his own, in every field in which he wrote. And his range, astonishingly wide, embraced theory of knowledge and philosophy of science, cosmology, Einsteinian relativity, quantum physics, probability theory, mathematics, logic, language, psychology, education, history, sociology, politics – and a whole host of other things, too, from the theory of evolution to music. He was a passionate scholar in the history of ideas. After The Open Society, Platonic exegesis was never the same again. In his late eighties he was publishing scholarly articles about the pre-Socratic philosophers, and in 1998 these articles were published in a book with the title The World of Parmenides. And at the same time as writing those articles he was continuing to publish original contributions to probability theory, which he was still doing even in 1994, the year of his death at the age of 92.

In all these widely differing fields his work had a certain method of approach in common. This is illuminating in itself, and intimately related to his general philosophy. He would start by identifying a worthwhile problem – not just any problem but one that was either of practical importance or of serious theoretical interest; and he would try to get it really clear to himself what it was and why it was a problem. He would then examine and evaluate the proposed solutions to this problem put forward by major contributors in the field, seeing what could be learnt from them and also where and why they fell short. He would then, in the light of this critical discussion, put forward his own solution. Then he would critically evaluate his own solution, putting it to the test in various ways and considering the arguments that could be brought against it, modifying it where necessary. Finally, having got his proposed solution into its most effective form, he would re-examine the problem-situation in the light of the new position reached.

One thing this schema brings out is the organic relationship between his criticism of others and his putting forward of his own ideas. This is an exceptionally striking feature of all his work – but not all readers have got from it what they should have done. For instance, generations of students have plundered The Open Society for its magnificent criticisms of Plato and Marx without reading the book as a whole, and therefore without even realizing that these criticisms are being put forward as part of the logical preliminary to an exposition of Popper's positive proposals about personal freedom, tolerance, democracy, and the need to base social policy on critical rationality; and that it is these positive proposals that constitute the primary aim of the book. Some of these people then go through the rest of their lives thinking that they have read The Open Society, and thinking that what it is, is a critique of Plato and Marx.

This methodological approach, which confers a certain unity on all of Popper's work in spite of the variety of its subject matter, is rooted in his theory of knowledge, and of the growth of knowledge; and it is this that is really foundational to his thinking, and the ultimate source of its unity. It is to this that we must now turn.

Descartes's work had the effect of placing the question "What can I know?" at the centre of Western Philosophical enquiry. Is there anything I can know for certain? How? And how will I know that I do know it for certain, even if I do? This pursuit of certainty governed both science and philosophy for three hundred years or more, well into the 20th century. Bertrand Russell began his intellectual career by trying to put mathematics on a foundation of certainty, and then moved from there to philosophy by trying to do the same thing for our empirical knowledge. The Logical Positivists were trying to find a rational demonstration of the certainty of scientific knowledge. And in each case this was what they described themselves as doing; it was their own conception of their task.

In most people's view the biggest single breakthrough in scientific knowledge that has ever occurred was that brought about by Newton. The way Newton's discoveries appeared for a very long time was expressed in two lines by the poet Alexander Pope:

"Nature and Natures laws lay hid in night:
God said, Let Newton be! And all was light."

Newton's laws were thought to be, as Pope said, laws of Nature; and they were taught as such in schools and colleges for over two hundred years. They revealed to us the truth about our cosmic situation, from the motions of the planets to the movements of the tides. Machines were constructed in accordance with the principles of Newtonian mechanics, and these principles were to provide the Industrial Revolution with its most essential theoretical foundations. Millions of times a day Newton's laws were being confirmed by being put to practical use, which showed that they worked. If anything was knowledge, this was, the most conclusively secured, the most certain knowledge that human beings had ever acquired.

Inevitably, this had profound and extensive consequences for philosophy. We human beings had always known what our own subjective experience was like, because it was what we had immediate knowledge of. But now, in addition to that, people thought that with Newton they had acquired objective knowledge of what the external world is like: it is as Newtonian science reveals it to be. What, then, is the relationship between the two – what is the relationship of our knowledge and experience to the world – and how is it to be accounted for? This question set the central task of epistemology from Newton to the twentieth century. It was thought that whatever account we give of human knowledge, it needs to have reality at both ends of it, so to speak: both the causes and the outcomes have to be accounted for in terms of a reality that is objectively given to us. Reality gives rise to experience and knowledge in us, in ways we want to be able to give a rational account of; and that knowledge, at least, if not always our subjective experience, has to match the objective reality of the world as it is revealed to us by science – and we want to be able to demonstrate that it does, and so to validate our knowledge.

The first philosopher of genius to respond directly to Newton's work was John Locke, who gave an account of knowledge along these lines. It is significant that his masterpiece was entitled An Essay Concerning Human Understanding – for it was not the world he was trying to give an account of but our understanding of the world, human knowledge. And of course he encountered profound difficulties, and a line of succession came into being that thought of itself as such, passing from Locke through Berkeley and Hume to Kant and Schopenhauer, addressing itself to the central question: How is it possible for us to have the knowledge that we do have of the world as revealed to us by science?

Locke and Hume, at least, were in many ways ahead of their time in realizing that human knowledge is not characterized by deductive certainty, nor indeed inductive certainty either, but this seemed to them a terrible problem. In Locke's case it had creative consequences in the political philosophy he formulated in organic interrelationship with his epistemology: our lack of certainty as to the knowledge we have is made by him into an argument for toleration, because it means we are never justified in imposing our views on others by force. The connection is brought out clearly in such passages as this: "For where is the man that has incontestable evidence of the truth of all that he holds, or of the falsehood of all he condemns, or can say that he has examined to the bottom all his own, or other men's opinions? The necessity of believing without knowledge, lay often upon very slight grounds, in this fleeting state of action and blindness we are in, should make us more busy and careful to inform ourselves than to constrain others." Thus this philosopher who is generally, and in my opinion rightly, regarded as the founder of the liberal tradition in political philosophy was directed into the very heart of his liberalism by his epistemology, and would have been so directed regardless of other considerations.

Within the world of professional philosophy Locke is thought of primarily as the founding father of modern empiricism, though in the world outside philosophy, his greatest impact has been in the field of social and political ideas. The Founding Fathers of the United States of America had Locke and his principles consciously in mind, and made frequent references to them, when they drew up the American Constitution. Voltaire was throughout his adult life an effective propagandist, and a propagandist of genius, for the ideas of Newton and Locke in France, and in Continental Europe generally. And in Britain itself the continuing influence of Lockean liberalism has been profound.

You will have guessed already, I am sure, that my recalling this period in the history of Western philosophy has a purpose to do with Karl Popper; and you may even have guessed what the purpose is. I think that the most revealing way to locate Popper in the general picture of philosophy's history is to see him as standing in a similar sort of relationship to the twentieth-century revolutions in science as Locke and his successors did to the Newtonian revolution. Einstein's theories were incompatible with Newton's, yet from the beginning no intellectually serious person could deny that they were worthy of consideration. But this alone meant that Newton's laws were not certain; might possibly be inaccurate. Einstein's theories laid themselves nakedly open to refutation by predicting consequences incompatible with Newton; but as experimental evidence accumulated it unmistakably favoured Einstein. In 1926 an English wit called J.C. Squire added a couplet to the one I quoted earlier from Alexander Pope, making four-line verse that new reads in toto:

"Nature and Nature's laws lay hid in night:
God said, Let Newton be! And all was light.
It did not last: the Devil howling Ho!
Let Einstein be! Restored the status quo"

The young Popper was fascinated by these events, and intellectually thrilled by them. And he saw that they had seismic implications for philosophy. First of all, Hume's point about the invalidity of induction was brought home to him in its full force. Newton's laws had been corroborated millions of times a day for over two hundred years, and yet still they turned out to be inaccurate. Popper realized that if one asked oneself what amount of observational evidence would have finally secured the certain truth of Newton's laws, the answer was "None". It is logically impossible that any unrestrictedly universal statement about the world, such as a scientific law, can ever be known with certainty to be true. But this meant that the pursuit of certainty that had governed Western science and philosophy from Descartes to Russell was a pursuit of the logically unattainable. The whole thing was a gigantic error, and had to be renounced. Knowledge as standardly defined, namely "justified true belief", was not available to us in science, because although some of our beliefs might be true none of them could ever be justified. The most we could ever do, as in the case of Einstein and Newton, was to justify our preference for one theory or set of theories over another; but this was not at all the same thing as justifying belief in the successor theory as being true. On the contrary, that would now be in the same case as the theory it had displaced. Interestingly, Einstein himself fully understood this. He realized that his theories relativity, though preferable to Newton's theories, were themselves not the last word, and he spent the last 20 years of his life in search of a better theory that would replace them. And Popper perceived that this was how scientific knowledge grows. It is not the case, as for hundreds of years people had believed, that the growth of our scientific knowledge consists in the perpetual addition of new certainties to an evergrowing body of existing ones: it consists in the overthrow of existing theories, and their replacement by better theories. And since no theory can ever be finally justified, this is a process that logically has no end. Our scientific knowledge is always fallible, always corrigible, constantly being superseded. The fact is immediately obvious, once we look, that every single one of the major sciences has not just grown but has radically changed in the course of the 20th century, and that comparatively little of what was "known" in the sciences in previous centuries is still regarded as completely valid.

It needs to be stressed at this point that Popper was in no sense whatever an idealist. He believed unequivocally that reality exists independently of us. Reality is not a product of the human mind – but knowledge is. What we call our knowledge can only ever be our theories. And it can never be proved that a theory wholly and completely corresponds to reality, though we may have good grounds for believing that theory B is nearer to whatever the truth is than theory A. This means that Popper is not in any sense a relativist either, because he believes that we can and usually do have good grounds for preferring the theories we accept to those we reject. How we arrived at the theories we prefer is literally of no significance, except perhaps historically, or psychologically: if a theory can be shown to be preferable to the reigning theory then we are justified by that fact (and could be justified by no other) in preferring it, and provisionally adopting it until a still better theory comes along. What "better" means in these circumstances may depend on the problem-situation, but usually it means either that theory B yields more accurate predictions than theory A or that theory B accounts for everything theory A can account for plus things that theory A fails to account for. In either case it means that theory B better withstands the tests of confrontation with reality than theory A, usually by making more, or more accurate, predictions. It is in this way that observation, experiment, measurement and so on come into a valid account of the rationale of science: not that they give rise to our theories, but that our theories, no matter how they are arrived at, have to be stable, once formulated, to withstand testing by means of them. For although our theories cannot be verified by observation, they may be falsified by observation: although no number of observations of white swans will ever verify the truth of the statement "All swans are white", one single observation of a black swan refutes it. This means that although unrestrictedly general empirical statements are not verifiable they are nevertheless testable; and that is utterly crucial. In fact, it was empirical testability that became Popper's criterion of demarcation between science and non-science.

In this way Popper dissolved the traditional problem of induction. Induction had become a crux in philosophy because people for a long time believed that our empirical knowledge must start from observation and experience; and the problem then became how to get from individual observation statements, however numerous, to unrestrictedly general statements – and of course there is no way of doing so that is justifiable in logic. Popper disposed of this problem by denying the premise. He denied that we must, or indeed even that we can, base our unrestrictedly general theories on the observation of particular instances. Some of his critics, unable to deny this, have tried to insist that we can nevertheless justify our acceptance of whatever theory we do embrace only by procedures in which induction plays a role: but to say this is already to have forgotten that Popper has denied that acceptance of the truth of a theory can ever be justified; the most that can be justified is a preference for one theory over another.

Thus Popper put forward an utterly transformed conception of the nature of science, compared with what had gone before, denying both of what had been thought to be its two salient features, namely certainty in its outcomes and induction in its methods, yet without being a relativist. What had become the conventional wisdom in the empiricist tradition – and this included both the positivists and the Logical Positivists – about the way science advances, and knowledge grows, had seen scientific method as starting from observation and measurement, and the accumulation of empirical data. Then, it was thought, by means of inductive logic we generalize from these to form hypotheses of a lawlike character. We then seek to verify our hypotheses, usually by devising crucial experiments to do so. If we succeed in verifying a lawlike hypothesis we have discovered a new scientific law. Popper rejected this whole framework from beginning to end. We begin, he said, not with observation but with a problem or set of problems, usually presented to us by a rebuff to our existing theory or expectations, though it doesn't actually matter how. We try to think of a way of solving our problem, and we come up with a tentative possible solution. We then try our solution out to see if it works: we devise critical tests for it, both theoretically and practically, and amend it in the light of these tests. Even so, we more often than not find that our proposed solution can't be made to work, so we have to start looking for another one. But this whole process is teaching us more than we understood before about the nature of the problem, and it may help us eventually to find a solution that does work. If we do, our new theory or explanation replaces our previous theory or expectations, and we carry on from there in the new situation – until we encounter the next problem. The whole process is problem-led, not observation-led. Our knowledge consists of explanations, and our explanatory theories are arrived at not by induction but by the self-critical use of an informed imagination. The whole approach is radically different from traditional empiricism, which now seems impoverished beside it. The name Popper gave to it was "critical rationalism", though it does not matter what we call it. When he had formulated it, Popper found that Einstein was already in at least partial agreement with him. In 1935 Einstein wrote a letter to Popper, which is now published as an appendix to The Logic of Scientific Discovery, in which he says: "Altogether I really do not at all like the now fashionable 'positivistic' tendency of clinging to what is observable...I think (like you, by the way) that theory cannot be fabricated out of the results of observation, but that it can only be invented." However, Einstein had come nowhere near to developing an equivalent to Popper's critical method.

Popper's earliest and most seminal work consists in unpacking the implications of this wholly new view of the nature of science that he was putting forward. And many Nobel Prize winners in the sciences have since agreed with one of their number, Peter Medawar, in saying that it constitutes the best philosophy of science there has ever been. But, of course, our scientific knowledge, for all its fallibility, is still the most reliable knowledge we possess; so if it is shown to be inherently uncertain, what does this have to say for the rest of our knowledge? Popper's philosophy of science thus had profound implications for theory of knowledge in general, implications that he himself worked out in an unusually full and rich manner. He argued that all empirical knowledge of a general character is conjectural, and must be open to refutation by experience if it is to be of any use to us; that a justified general belief is something we simply never have.

In the context of this article it is impossible to look at the connecting tissue between Popper's ideas, to examine how one follows from another, or develops out of another, or leads to another. Nor is there space to consider objections to his views. But in his own expositions he does all these things with exceptional fullness. And in the course of his doing so not only did the revolutionary philosophy of science with which he began open completely new vistas in general epistemology, but he then found, as Locke had done before him, that his epistemology led him to take up positions in social and political theory. And although, again like Locke, he remains best known within the world of professional philosophy for his epistemology (in Popper's case his philosophy of science especially), outside academe he is better known and more influential for his political philosophy.

It was some years before he himself realized that his epistemology committed him to certain fundamental political and social views, but then he saw that his disbelief in the logical availability of certainty undermined authoritarian claims. A social policy is an empirical hypothesis – "if we do such and such things, such and such consequences will follow" – and it is a matter of common observation that such predictions are almost never faultlessly accurate. They can nearly always be improved by criticism. Even then they more often than not have unintended consequences in the form of unexpected side-effects. The sooner these are identified, the greater can be the saving of resources, whether of people, money or time; but again that means criticism. So both before and after the implementation of policies, criticism is the chief agent of their improvement. Thus, societies in which criticism of government policies is allowed are almost bound to be more successful in achieving the aims of the policy makers than societies in which it is not. And this is true without making any judgments about the moral value of freedom of speech. From this sort of starting point Popper went on to put a highly practical as well as extraordinarily powerful case for what he called "openness" in social affairs, a concept that includes high levels of freedom and tolerance for the individual. I believe, as do many others, that it is the best case for what we normally think of as liberal democracy that has ever been put. And it completely rejects the still widely held view that the best available form of government for an underdeveloped society is some sort of benign authoritarianism.

People who mistakenly think of The Open Society as being a critique of Plato and Marx may imagine that, now that Marxism is no longer so much of a live issue, Popper's political writing is losing its urgency of application and acquiring a dated air. But in fact his positive proposals in political philosophy are of the utmost relevance and value, indeed urgency today in the great majority of the world's countries that are not open societies. And parallel claims hold good right across the board of this philosophy. It is a mistake to think that now that Logical Positivism is no longer espoused by anyone, or now that few people any longer regard Freudian psychology as a genuine science, or now that people generally are coming to realize that science itself does not consist of unchanging certainties, or now that analytic philosophy has lost its near-monopoly position in the English-speaking world, Popper's philosophy no longer meets felt needs. This is to see him only as a critic. He was indeed a great critic, the outstanding one of the 20th century in philosophy, but in addition to that he was a great original, creative and constructive thinker, and there is still a huge amount to be got out of the development of his positive ideas.

Popper's Early Work on the Theory of Knowledge[*]

Troels Eggers Hansen

On June 30th, 1932, a young schoolteacher in Vienna sent off a heavy parcel. The parcel contained a large manuscript – about 400 typed pages. The parcel was addressed to the Viennese poet and cultural historian Egon Friedell[1], and the schoolteacher was the 30 year old Karl Popper who had just completed the first volume of an epistemological treatise in two volumes: *Die beiden Grundprobleme der Erkenntnistheorie*[2].

In the enclosed letter to Egon Friedell, Popper describes his book as follows:

»Mein Buch ist eine Erkenntnistheorie, genauer: eine Methodenlehre. Es ist ein Kind der Zeit, ein Kind der Krise, – wenn auch vor allem der Krise der *Physik*. Es behauptet die *Permanenz der Krise*; wenn es recht hat, so ist die Krise der Normalzustand einer hochentwickelten rationalen Wissenschaft.«[3]

The purpose of sending the manuscript to Egon Friedell was to receive his opinion. Of course, a favourable opinion from Egon Friedell would make a good impression on publishers; whether he ever sent Popper such an opinion, I do not know.

Popper's manuscript was also read by several philosophers: Herbert Feigl, Rudolf Carnap, Moritz Schlick, Philipp Frank, Hans Hahn, Otto Neurath, Viktor Kraft, and also by Heinrich Gomperz. Popper received favourable opinions, and he approached some publishers. Heinrich Gomperz wrote a long letter to *Mohr Verlag* in Tübingen. But all attempts were fruitless. Until 1979, *Die beiden Grundprobleme* remained unpublished. In October 1979, all the parts of the manuscript that could be found were published by *Mohr Verlag*[4] in Tübingen – the publishing firm that 47 years earlier had declined to publish the book.

In the following, I shall tell you the strange story of *Die beiden Grundprobleme*; and I shall also give you an outline of the contents of the book.

In the theory of knowledge, there are, according to Popper, *two* fundamental problems: the *problem of induction* and the *problem of demarcation*. These two problems – die beiden Grundprobleme der Erkenntnistheorie – can be described in the following way:

The *problem of induction* is the question about the *validity* (or about the *justification*) of the universal statements of the empirical sciences. It is the question, whether empirical statements, that is, statements about reality, based upon experience, can have universal validity.[5]

The *problem of demarcation* is the question about a criterion demarcating the empirical sciences from non-empirical fields. It is the question, whether there is a criterion which qualifies certain statements or systems of statements as empirical and others as non-empirical.[6]

The first volume of *Die beiden Grundprobleme* contains a thorough discussion of the *problem of induction*. Popper's conclusion is clear and unambiguous:

»... es gibt keine Induktion im erkenntnistheoretischen Sinn.«[7]

»Der Induktivismus ist nicht anderes als eine (primitive) Lösung des Abgrenzungsproblems: Aus Angst vor der Metaphysik (die Angst ist nur zu berechtigt, solange man nicht über ein brauchbares Abgrenzungskriterium verfügt) klammert sich der (induktivistisch orientierte) Empirist möglichst fest an die unmittelbaren Daten der Erfahrung.«[8]

In the first volume, Popper indicates his own criterion of demarcation; but a thorough discussion of the *problem of demarcation* – showing that his own criterion is both adequate and very useful – had to be postponed to the second volume.

A meeting in 1929 or in 1930 was to be of great importance to Popper's work. It was a meeting with Herbert Feigl. The two young philosophers met for the first time and »spent a whole night in a most exciting discussion«[9]. Feigl found Popper's ideas »important, almost revolutionary«, and he encouraged Popper to publish what he has written. Popper says that this »meeting ... became decisive for [his] whole life [and] without encouragement from Herbert Feigl it is unlikely that [he] should ever have written a book«[10].

Popper wrote the first drafts of *Die beiden Grundprobleme* pretty quickly, and as soon as he had a section typed he showed it to Robert Lammer, his friend and former colleague at the *Pedagogic Institute of the City of Vienna*[11]. Lammer was a very »conscientious and critical reader ... he challenged every point which he did not find crystal clear«[12].

When Popper prepared his manuscript, Robert Lammer was of great help to him. When – many, many years later – I prepared my edition of *Die beiden Grundprobleme*, Robert Lammer was to be of great help to me, too.

To the best of my knowledge nothing remains of the first drafts of *Die beiden Grundprobleme*; and I do not know more about these drafts than what I have just told you.

The version of the first volume of *Die beiden Grundprobleme* which has been preserved, seems to have been written between February 1931 and the summer of 1932[13].

What follows is an outline – admittedly, a *very* rough outline – of the contents of the *first volume*.

The starting point of Popper's discussion of the *problem of induction* is Hume's Argument. Hume

»wies nach, daß jeder Versuch einer *induktiven Verallgemeinerung* einem Zirkelschluß erliegen muß.«[14]

Hume showed that natural laws cannot be justified by observations. Instead of demonstrating the defeat by a circular inference, Popper showed that every *inductive generalization* will be defeated by an *infinite regress*[15].

There seems to be no gap in Hume's argument and this result leads to the question how one should now understand natural laws which are universal empirical statements?[16] A discussion of the possible answers to this question is the topic of the first volume of *Die beiden Grundprobleme*.

In his discussion of the problem of induction, Popper strives to discuss *all* possible answers to the question raised by Hume's argument; and he proceeds here in a very *systematic* fashion. The various answers or positions are organized according to the following groups:

1. Die Normalsatzpositionen
2. Die Wahrscheinlichkeitspositionen
3. Die Scheinsatzpositionen.

All three groups of positions agree with respect to the type of validity of the *singular* empirical statements; but they disagree as to the type of validity of the *universal* empirical statements.

The *singular* empirical statements – the basic or observational statements – have a *normal* type of validity; they are ›vollentscheidbar‹ – they are fully decidable: »... if they are true, their truth is *decidable*, and, if they are false, their falsity is *decidable*; that is, decidable by *experience*.«[17]

According to the first group of positions, the ›*Normalsatzpositionen*‹, *all* empirical statements have a *normal* type of validity; *all* empirical statements are fully decidable. If there are any *universal* natural laws, that is, if there are any *universal* empirical statements, then these statements – like singular empirical statements – must have a normal type of validity. Whether there are any *universal* empirical statements – this is a question on which the various normal-statement positions disagree.

According to the second group of positions, the ›*Wahrscheinlichkeitspositionen*‹, the universal empirical statements do not have a normal type of validity; instead they have a *probability* value.

According to the third group of positions, the ›*Scheinsatzpositionen*‹, the so-called universal empirical statements are not statements at all; they are *pseudo-statements*. The natural laws are not statements, but they are »Anweisungen zur Bildung von Aussagen«[18]; they are »instructions for the formation of statements«, that is, instructions for the formation of *singular* empirical statements.

The first group of positions, the ›*Normalsatzpositionen*‹, consists of three positions only: *naive inductivism*, *strict positivism*, and *apriorism*.

According to *naive inductivism*, there is a method – a so-called "scientific" method – that enables us to establish true universal laws; according to this position, universal natural laws are justifiable, that is, justifiable by experience. *Naive inductivism* has, however, been defeated by Hume's argument, and it must be considered untenable.

Thus, within the *normal-statement positions* we are left with two positions only: *strict positivism* and *apriorism*. There are only two possibilities: either one denies that there are universal empirical statements, or one accepts the existence of *a priori* synthetic statements.

According to *strict positivism* (not to be confused with *logical* positivism), there are no universal empirical statements; natural laws are only *summary reports* of our observations[19].

According to *apriorism* – the position of Kant – there are universal empirical statements. They are *a priori* synthetic statements, and these »most general laws of nature are ›quite the same‹ as the most general formal conditions of experience[20].

The two remaining groups of positions – the ›*probability positions*‹ and the ›*pseudostatement positions*‹ – are more difficult to describe. About these positions, Popper says:

»Die Wahrscheinlichkeitspositionen und noch mehr die Scheinsatzpositionen Haben sich als so unfertige, so unbestimmte, ich möchte fast sagen, molluskoide Gebilde erwiesen, dass die Kritik sich vorerst bemühen [muss], ihnen etwas festere Umrisse zu geben.«[21]

> »Es ist wichtig, das festzustellen; denn Teile meiner Polemik werden sich aus diesem Grund vielleicht nur gegen imaginäre Gegner richten.«[22]

I refrain from giving you a summary of all the various positions and of the criticisms leveled against them by Popper[23]. I cannot possible do justice to his very severe criticisms of *logical positivism*; nor can I possibly do justice to his very thorough criticisms of Kant's *transcendental deduction* and *transcendental idealism* or to the subsequent criticisms of *Leonard Nelson* and of *Jakob Friedrich Fries* – criticisms that form a whole and lead to Popper's theory of the empirical basis.

For my purpose – to give an outline of the book – suffice it to say that *all* positions have to be rejected. either because they turn out to be logically untenable: like *naive inductivism* they are defeated by an *infinite regress*; or they have to be rejected, because they turn out to be in disagreement with »*the actual procedures of science*«[24]; or because they turn out to be dependent on a concept of meaning that is not open to discussion[25], that is, because it turns out that these positions are immunized against criticism by a retreat to dogmatism.

Referring to these last positions, Popper concludes his long and very detailed discussions of the *problem of induction* by stating:

> »So landet das schwankende Schiff des Induktivismus nach mancherlei Irrfahrt zwischen der Skylla des unendlichen Regresses und der Charybdis des Apriori im sicheren Hafen des Dogmas.«[26]

Thus, all the various positions – all the various answers to the question raised by Hume's argument – have been shown to be defective; and there seems to be no solution to the problem of induction.

But there *is* a solution to the problem of induction which consists in a *downright rejection* of inductivism. This is Popper's solution.

Like all positions within the three groups of positions stated above (normal-statement positions, probability positions and pseudo-statement positions) Popper's position is an answer to the question raised by Hume's argument. Considering that every *inductive generalization* will be defeated by an *infinite regress*, one can now return to the question: How can one understand natural laws, that is, universal empirical statements?

The difference between Popper's position and all other positions can be illustrated by returning to the normal-statement positions. According to the *normal-statement positions*, *all* empirical statements must be *fully* decidable. If there are any universal empirical statements, then these statements – like singular empirical statements – must have a normal type of validity and therefore must be *fully* decidable. Here we get to the root of the matter: it is the idea, that *all genuine* statements must be *fully* decidable[27] which prevents a solution to the problem of induction.

Popper's position is *not* an inductivist position; he does not accept what he calls the »*Grundthese des Induktivismus*«:

»Alle legitimen Sätze der Wissenschaft müssen sich auf elementare Erfahrungssätze zurückführen lassen ...«[28]

Popper's position is a genuine *deductivist* position[29] that may be characterized asfollows:

Natural laws, that is, universal empirical statements, are legitimate statements, but they are not ›*vollentscheidbar*‹, they are not fully decidable. Natural laws are ›*teilentscheidbar*‹, they are only *partially decidable*. Natural laws are not verifiable, they are *only falsifiable*; thus, if they are true, their truth *cannot* be decided, but if they are false, their falsity can be decided by experience, by demonstrating the falsity of some of the prognoses deduced from theses laws.

Popper's solution of the problem of induction leads to a *criterion* demarcating the empirical sciences from non-empirical fields and thus also offers a solution of the problem of demarcation. It is the basis of Poppers theory of methodology and his view of science as *conjectures and refutations*.

Here we have to leave the first volume of *Die beiden Grundprobleme* and turn to the *second volume* which dealt with the problem of demarcation. The fate of this volume is a complicated and sad story and I cannot possibly give you an outline of its contents.

The manuscript of the second volume seems to have been lost but in the first volume and in the remaining fragments of the second volume there are references that seem to indicate that the second volume of *Die beiden Grundprobleme* contained, or was to contain, the following three parts in that order[30]

Untersuchungen über das Abgrenzungsproblem
Übergang zur Methodentheorie
Grundzüge der allgemeinen Methodentheorie

The second part, *Übergang zur Methodentheorie*, appears to be almost completely preserved. This ›Übergang‹ deals with the ›konventionalistischen Einwand gegen die Falsifizierbarkeit‹; and it emphasizes the importance of a theory of methodology.

In the following, I tell what I know about the manuscript of the second volume and I shall also relate the story of its fate as I got to know it.

In the spring of 1932, Popper commenced his work on the second volume of *Die beiden Grundprobleme*. I do not know if he ever completed this volume, but I do know that early in 1934, it was *almost* completed.

On February 3, 1934, Popper sent a letter to the English philosopher L. Susan Stebbing. Answering a letter from Professor Stebbing, he writes:

»Sie fragen, ob der 2. Band des Buches bereits existiert und ob die fehlenden Kapitel des 1. Bandes, den Sie gelesen haben, bereits geschrieben sind. Der 2. Band ist fast fertiggestellt, aber einige Stellen müssen noch umgearbeitet werden. Der 1. Band, den Sie in einer Abschrift haben, wurde von mir vor mehr als zwei Jahren fertiggestellt. Sie werden es verstehen, daß ich inzwischen mehrere wichtige Verbesserungen auch an diesem 1. Band vorgenommen habe. Einige Verbesserungen, die ich noch vornehmen will, sind noch nicht ganz fertig. Das letzte Kapitel, nach dem Sie fragen, ist bereits geschrieben.«[31]

Die beiden Grundprobleme was never to be published according to the original plan. In its place, Popper had to publish quite a different book: *Logik der Forschung*. His letter of February 3, 1934, to Professor Stebbing contains a very early account of this story:

»Sie wünschen, darüber unterrichtet zu werden, was für Schritte ich wegen einer Veröffentlichung bisher unternommen habe. Ich berichte Ihnen gerne darüber: Die gegenwärtigen Verhältnisse in Deutschland und in Oesterreich sind für eine Veröffentlichung sehr ungünstig, dennoch habe ich einen Verleger gefunden und zwar den Verlag Julius Springer in Wien. Wegen der ungünstigen Verhältnisse will jedoch der Verlag Springer kein so umfangreiches Buch drucken. Ich mußte also das Buch sehr stark kürzen. Den ganzen 1. Band, den Sie kennen, habe ich dabei überhaupt weggelassen, und aus dem 2. Band einen kurzen Auszug gemacht (ungefähr 200 Seiten), der nur die wichtigsten erkenntnislogischen Ueberlegungen und Anwendungen enthält. Es ist auf diese Weise eigentlich ein ganz neues Buch entstanden. Der Titel dieses neuen Buches wird wahrscheinlich lauten: ›Logik der Forschung‹. Es wird in der von Prof. Schlick herausgegebenen Sammlung ›Schriften zur wissenschaftlichen Weltauffassung‹ im Mai[32] dieses Jahres erscheinen ... Das neue Buch ... wird fast nur logische Fragen enthalten. Von einer Kritik der verschiedenen erkenntnistheoretischen Richtungen, insbesondere von der Kritik des Positivismus wird kaum ein Wort drin stehen.«[33]

Now, what happened to the manuscript of the second volume of *Die beiden Grundprobleme* and to some of the other early manuscripts of Popper's?

In 1972, when I started my editorial work on *Die beiden Grundprobleme*, I had at my disposal two copies of the first volume: the top-copy and a carbon-copy. I also had labout 500 typed pages enclosed in a folder labeled: *Logik der Forschung: Ur-Version*.

In January 1972, this ›*Ur-Version*‹ turned up in Popper's house in Penn. The folder contained a chaotic mixture of fragments of the second volume of *Die beiden Grundprobleme* and of one of the earlier versions of *Logik der Forschung*. All the fragments of the second volume, which was published 1979, come from this folder.

In 1971, Popper had told me that in the beginning of 1937 – just before he and his wife left Vienna for New Zealand – he deposited a wardrobe full of manuscripts in the apartment of Otto Haas, one of his friends. Seven years later, Haas was executed by the Nazis.

After the war, a search for the deposited manuscripts was made, but the second volume did not turn up.

In the assumption that I had at my disposal all the extant manuscripts relating to *Die beiden Grundprobleme*, I carried on my editorial work. Then, in 1974, something related to our story happened in Vienna. In his house, Robert Lammer – Popper's old friend of whom I have already told you – came across a *second* carbon-copy of the first volume of *Die beiden Grundprobleme*. A new search for manuscripts started, many, many letters were exchanged, and – as a result of the search – a *third* carbon-copy of the first volume, some minor manuscripts, and various old letters turned up; and a strange story was revealed. The following is a summary of the story I got to know[34].

In the beginning of 1937, when Popper and his wife left for New Zealand, they had to leave a great variety of things behind, unsorted. In order to arrive at the commencement of the New Zealand academic year (in March), they had to leave Vienna within four weeks from Popper's appointment, on Christmas Eve, 1936, to a lectureship in Canterbury University College, Christchurch. There simply was no time for anything.[35] As already mentioned, Popper deposited a wardrobe full of manuscripts in the apartment of his friend Otto Haas which was situated in his mother's flat, and she took care of her son's belongings after his death, until she herself died several years after the war.

In 1953, Paul Feyerabend visited London, and before he returned to Vienna, Popper asked him to try to fetch the deposited manuscripts. Back in Vienna, Feyerabend went to Robert Lammer and together they visited old Frau Haas. They were shown into Otto Haas' apartment, and as they pulled out the drawers of his writing table a lot of manuscripts appeared.

While searching the drawers, they found a parcel labeled *Für Robert Lammer!! Dr. Karl Popper*. A little later one more parcel turned up. Also this parcel was labeled *Für Robert Lammer!! Dr. Karl Popper*. The two parcels were exactly alike. The first parcel was given to Robert Lammer; the second parcel was not. This was a disaster. The second parcel was put back in one of the drawers without further inspection and has since disappeared.[36]

In the weeks or months following that visit, Feyerabend several times visited Frau Haas; and she gave him many (perhaps all) of the manuscrips deposited early in 1937. Owing to some misunderstandings not all of these manuscripts were sent on to Popper. In 1975, Feyerabend still had some of Popper's early manuscripts, and he kindly sent me all the material to be found in his files. In this material, I found a few minor manuscripts and some old letters; for instance, the letter of June 30th, 1932, to Egon Friedell and the letter to Professor Stebbing I have just quoted.[37]

Some twenty years after the visit to Frau Haas, Robert Lammer came across the parcel that she did give him. This parcel – that contains a *second* carbon-copy of the first volume of *Die beiden Grundprobleme* – was sent on to me. About half a year later, Robert Lammer sent me a *third* carbon-copy of the first volume that he had just received from Feyerabend.[38]

What has happened to the parcel Frau Haas did *not* give to Robert Lammer? Nobody seems to know. The only thing I can tell you is, that Popper was convinced that it contained the manuscript of the second volume of *Die beiden Grundprobleme*.[39]

When I started my editorial work, I had a dream: a dream of finding the missing second volume, so that I could bring out a complete edition of *Die beiden Grundprobleme der Erkenntnistheorie*. I still have that dream, but it is very unlikely that it will come true.

As I wrote in my *Nachwort* to the book I did bring out:

»... [es muß] leider ... als wahrscheinlich angesehen werden, daß Band II jetzt als Folge von einer Reihe unglücklicher Mißverständnisse verlorengegangen ist.«[40]

The fact that in the thirties *Die beiden Grundprobleme* was not published according to the original plan, is a tragedy. And it is a pity, that the publication of the remaining parts of *Die beiden Grundprobleme* took place many years after the abbreviated version, *Logik der Forschung*, had been translated into English and, naturally, had become the standard work on the philosophy of Popper.

Of course, *The Logic of Scientific Discovery*[41] is of fundamental importance for an understanding of his philosophy. But in order to understand the background of Popper's philosophy of science and to get a good grasp of his ideas, I recommend to prospective students of Popper to start by reading *Die beiden Grundprobleme*, and *then* to proceed to reading the *Logik der Forschung*[42]. *Die beiden Grundprobleme* is a model of careful discussions, and it is bursting with ideas.

I have only given you an outline of the contents of *Die beiden Grundprobleme* – very rough outline indeed. Outlining its contents, I had to refrain from mentioning some very important ideas. I did not mention Popper's clear distinction between the *psychology* of knowledge and the *theory* of knowledge – his *rejection of psychologism*. Nor did I mention the fundamental distinction between *singular* and *strictly universal* statements. To realize that this distinction is *unequivocal* – just as is the distinction between *individual* and *universal* concepts – is fundamental for an understanding of the problem of induction. The problem of induction »cannot even be formulated without this distinction«[43].

In the remaining fragments of the second volume of *Die beiden Grundprobleme*, the discussions of the distinction between *individual* and *universal* concepts are developed and lead to the idea of theories as nets – nets with which we seek to capture reality.[44] Our theories, our universal natural laws, and our universal concepts are indispensable to our attempts at capturing reality; but they can never capture reality completely:

»Wie fein wir auch das Netz spinnen, die Wirklichkeit ist immer noch feiner. Nur das Gröbste bleibt im Netz zurück.«[45]

This idea, I think, is the main reason why Popper, in *Die beiden Grundprobleme*, had chosen to quote as a motto the fifth *Dialogue*[46] of Novalis:

»Hypothesen sind Netze, nur der wird fangen, der auswirft ...«

I wish to thank Mrs. Melitta Mew for permitting me to quote two old letters of Popper's.

Notes

* On 30 October 1998, I held, at the University of Vienna, my Ringvorlesung on Popper's early work on the theory of Knowledge; and at that time, I concentrated on *Die beiden Grundprobleme der Erkenntnistheorie*. However, in order to get an understanding of Popper's early intellectual development a study of his articles and dissertations from the years before he embarked on writing *Die beiden Grundprobleme* is also of great importance. In 2006, the few published articles and the remaining manuscripts from the years 1925-1936 were made easily available by the publication of Karl Popper, *Frühe Schriften* (ed. by Troels Eggers Hansen; Karl Popper, *Gesammelte Werke in deutscher Sprache* 1, Tübingen: Mohr Siebeck). For a discussion of Popper's early work on the two fundamental problems of the theory of knowledge, see Troels Eggers Hansen, ›Which Came First, the Problem of Induction or the Problem of Demarcation?‹, in: *Karl Popper: A Centenary Assessment*, volume I (ed. by Ian Jarvie, Karl Milford, and David Miller, Aldershot: Ashgate, 2006), pp. 67-81.
1. Egon Friedell: 1878-1938.
2. The title is an allusion to Arthur Schopenhauer, *Die beiden Grundprobleme der Ethik, behandelt in zwei akademischen Preisschriften* ... (1841; 21860).
3. Cf. Karl Popper, *Die beiden Grundprobleme der Erkenntnistheorie* (1979; ^{2}1994), pp. XIV, 443. For the opposite view, cf. Thomas S. Kuhn, *The Structure of Scientific Revolutions* (1962; ^{2}1970).
4. J.C.B. Mohr (Paul Siebeck), Tübingen, 1979; 2. verbesserte Auflage, 1994. Forthcoming: 3. verbesserte Auflage (to be published as volume 2 of Karl Popper, *Gesammelte Werke in deutscher Sprache*, Tübingen: Mohr Siebeck).
5. Karl Popper, *op. cit.*, p. 349.
6. Karl Popper, *op. cit.*, p. 347.
7. Karl Popper, *op. cit.*, p. 327.
8. Karl Popper, *op. cit.*, p. 288.
9. Karl Popper, ›A Theorem on Truth-Content‹, in: *Mind, Matter, and Method: Essays in Philosophy and Science in Honor of Herbert Feigl*, edited by Paul K. Feyerabend and Grover Maxwell, 1966, p. 343.
10. Karl Popper, ›Intellectual Autobiography‹, in: *The Philosophy of Karl Popper* I., edited by Paul Arthur Schilpp, 1974, p. 65 (= Karl Popper, *Unended Quest: An Intellectual Autobiography*, 1976, pp. 82 f.).
11. ›Hochschulmäßige Lehrerbildungskurse‹ (1925-1927) am *Pädagogischen Institut der Stadt Wien*, Wien VII., Burggasse 14-16.
12. Karl Popper, *op. cit.*, p. 66 (= Karl Popper, *Unended Quest: An Intellectual Autobiography*, 1976, p. 83).
13. On February 13, 1931, Moritz Schlick's paper ›Die Kausalität in der gegenwärtigen Physik‹ was published in the weekly *Die Naturwissenschaften* (19. Jahrgang, Heft 7). In Popper's discussions of the problem of induction, Schlick's paper plays a *very* important part; and before February 13, 1931, he could not possibly have commenced his work. In the long Section 11 on Kant and Fries, a reference (Karl Popper, *Die beiden Grundprobleme der Erkenntnistheorie*, 1979, ^{2}1994, p. 121: note 53) seems to indicate that the first

volume must have been completed between late March 1932 and the summer of 1932 when Popper sent a copy of his manuscript to Egon Friedell and, in the Tyrolean Alps a few weeks later, showed another copy to Rudolf Carnap and to Herbert Feigl. (Karl Popper, ›Intellectual Autobiography‹, in: *The Philosophy of Karl Popper* I., edited by Paul Arthur Schilpp, 1974, p. 71 = Karl Popper, *Unended Quest: An Intellectual Autobiography*, 1976, pp. 89 f.; Karl Popper, ›Replies to My Critics‹, in: *The Philosophy of Karl Popper* II., edited by P.A. Schilpp, 1974, pp. 968 f.; Karl Popper, *Conjectures and Refutations*, 1963, pp. 253 f.) However, see this paper, text to note 31.

Die beiden Grundprobleme was typed by Popper's wife. In the early 1980s she told me that, when working on the manuscript, they often made excursions to the surroundings of Vienna. Popper carried the typewriter and, in the small restaurant where they used to have their meals, he was for that reason known as »the man with the gramophone«.

14 Karl Popper, *Die beiden Grundprobleme der Erkenntnistheorie* (1979; ^{2}1994), p. 33.

15 In a new footnote (added in1975), Popper remarks: »Der unendliche Regreß findet sich schon ganz explizit bei Hume.« See Karl Popper, *op. cit.*, p. 33: note *1.

Popper's demonstration of the *infinite regress* can be summarized as follows: What we get to know by observation is, that a number – a *finite* number – of singular empirical statements are true. This set of true statements is, however, not sufficient to justify an inductive generalization. In order to justify a set of observations being generalized into a universal law, we need a *principle of induction* that enables us to demonstrate the truth of that universal law – and this need for a principle of induction leads to an *infinite regress*. Whatever such a principle of induction is, it must be a universal empirical statement that says something about the lawlikeness or about the uniformity of nature. Thus, also a principle of induction has to be justified – and, like the natural laws, it has to be justified by observations, by singular empirical statements. That is, a *second order* principle of induction has to be introduced and to be justified – and so forth.

16 Karl Popper, *op. cit.*, p. 39.
17 Karl Popper, *op. cit.*, p. 42: note *1.
18 Moritz Schlick, ›Die Kausalität in der gegenwärtigen Physik‹, *Die Naturwissenschaften* 19 (Heft 7, 13. Februar 1931), p. 151. See also Karl Popper, *op. cit.*, Section 19.
19 Karl Popper, *op. cit.*, p. 43 f.
20 Immanuel Kant, *Prolegomena* (1783), § 36, p. 112. See also Karl Popper, *op. cit.*, p. 75.
21 Karl Popper, *op. cit.*, p. 254.
22 Karl Popper, *op. cit.*, p. 160.
23 One of the many issues discussed by Popper while dealing with the pseudo-statement positions (and also while dealing, in one of the remaining fragments of the second volume, with the problem of methodology) is the thesis that has later become known as the *Duhem-Quine-Thesis* (Karl Popper, *op. cit.*, pp. 259 ff., 390 ff.). Dudley Shapere seems to have failed to notice Popper's early discussions of Duhem when he writes (*Annals of Science* 54,

1997, p. 308): »Even Popper, when he learned of Duhem's objection (*after* having failed to notice it in the original edition of *Logik der Forschung* or in the original English translation), admitted that straightforward logical refutation of a hypothesis is not possible, ...« (my emphasis). A failure to notice Popper's rather detailed discussions of Duhem also seems to underlie the criticisms leveled against his »notion of falsifiability« by Ernan McMullin (*The British Journal for the Philosophy of Science* 48, 1997, p. 607).
24 Karl Popper, *op. cit.*, p. 263.
25 Cf. Karl Popper, *op. cit.*, pp. 294 ff.
26 Karl Popper, *op. cit.*, p. 299.
27 For the idea, that *all genuine* statements must be *fully* decidable, cf. Moritz Schlick, *op. cit.*, p. 156: »[Es ist] für eine echte Aussage wesentlich ..., daß sie prinzipiell endgültig verifizierbar oder falsifizierbar ist«. Cf. also Karl Popper, *op. cit.*, pp. 42, 301 ff.
28 Karl Popper, *op. cit.*, p. 288.
29 By their definition, the pseudo-statement positions seem to be deductivist positions, too. But this is not the case: »... der Terminus ›Anweisungen zur Bildung von Sätzen‹ gestattet nicht, Schlüsse darauf zu ziehen, wie diese Bildung vor sich gehen soll.« (Karl Popper, *op. cit.*, p. 269.)
30 See my ›Nachwort‹, Section 6, to Karl Popper, *op. cit.*
31 Hoover Institute Archives, Popper Papers (352, 15). For the manuscript of the first volume, cf. this paper, note 13.
32 *Logik der Forschung* was not to be published until *December*, 1934. See Karl Popper, Letter of December 6, 1934, to Werner Heisenberg, Hoover Institute Archives, Popper Papers (305, 32); cf. also Malachi H. Hacohen, ›Karl Popper, the Vienna Circle, and Red Vienna‹, *Journal of the History of Ideas* 59 (1998), p. 723: note 44; M. H. Hacohen, *Karl Popper: The Formative Years 1902-1945* (2000), p. 243 f. (See also Karl Popper, *Frühe Schriften, Gesammelte Werke* 1, 2006, Nr. *8*, note 6.)
For the story of *Logik der Forschung*, see Karl Popper, ›Intellectual Autobiography‹, in: *The Philosophy of Karl Popper* I., edited by Paul Arthur Schilpp, 1974, p. 67 (= Karl Popper, *Unended Quest: An Intellectual Autobiography*, 1976, p. 85). (See also Karl Popper, *Logik der Forschung*, 11. Auflage, ed. by Herbert Keuth, *Gesammelte Werke* 3, 2005, ›Nachwort des Herausgebers‹; as well as M. H. Hacohen, *op. cit.*, Chapter 6.)
33 Professor L. Susan Stebbing had suggested that an English translation of *Die beiden Grundprobleme* should be published, and she also seems to have found a translator (Miss M. Gabain?) willing to do the job. In his letter of February 3, 1934, Popper writes about this suggestion:
»Ich habe mich nun über Ihren Vorschlag, eine englische Uebersetzung erscheinen zu lassen, aus folgendem Grund sehr gefreut: Das Buch hat in seiner ursprünglichen Form, in der Sie es kennen, viele Vorzüge und ich würde mich nur sehr ungern dazu entschließen, den Plan ganz aufzugeben, das Buch (mit Verbesserungen) in der alten Form erscheinen zu lassen. Aber es ist gegenwärtig fast unmöglich, in Oesterreich oder Deutschland einen Verleger zu finden, der ein so umfangreiches philosophisches Buch veröffentlichen würde. Eine englische Uebersetzung ist daher die einzige Möglichkeit, das Buch, an dem ich viele Jahre gear-

beitet habe, in der Form erscheinen zu lassen, in der es entstanden ist und die ihm entspricht: als ein Buch über die Erkenntnistheorie.«
The letter from Professor Stebbing to Popper seems to have been lost.

34 For a fuller account of this sad story, see Karl Popper, *Frühe Schriften* (*Gesammelte Werke* 1, ed. by Troels Eggers Hansen, 2006), ›Nachwort des Herausgebers‹, Abschnitt *II*: ›Die Geschichte der frühen Manuskripte‹, pp. 511-521; see also Abschnitt *I*, pp.510 f.

35 Karl Popper, Letter of August 20, 1974, to Troels Eggers Hansen. See also Karl Popper, ›Intellectual Autobiography‹, in: *The Philosophy of Karl Popper* I., edited by Paul Arthur Schilpp, p. 88 (= Karl Popper, *Unended Quest: An Intellectual Autobiography*, 1976, pp. 110 f.).

36 Robert Lammer, Letter of November 30, 1975, to Troels Eggers Hansen.

37 Some of the material sent on to me from Professor Paul Feyerabend turned out to be very important for my editorial work, and I am grateful for his help.

38 Among the various old letters I received from Feyerabend, was a long letter [of 1932] from Karl Popper to [Julius] Kraft. From this letter it appears, that 4 – and *only* 4 – copies of the manuscript were made. I now had at my disposal all 4 copies: the top-copy and the 3 carbon-copies.

Without the assistance of Robert Lammer, the strange story of the disappearance of several of Popper's early manuscripts would never have been revealed. At the time the search was made, Robert Lammer and his wife were both very ill; nevertheless he tried hard to find the disappeared manuscripts – especially, the disappeared manuscript of the second volume of *Die beiden Grundprobleme*. He has written long and very informative letters about this sad affair both to Popper and to me.

I am also very grateful for the help I received from Popper and Jeremy Shearmur.

39 Robert Lammer, Letter of November 30, 1975, to Troels Eggers Hansen. Of course, unless this parcel (or some other piece of evidence) turns up, it is impossible to prove that this is actually the case. An examination of the parcel that Frau Haas did give Robert Lammer, shows, however, that the content of the disappeared parcel most probably was the manuscript of the second volume. The parcel that Frau Haas did give Robert Lammer, contained the manuscript of the first volume; each section of this manuscript was enclosed in folders numbered as follows:

$$11, 21, 31, \ldots, 481.$$

(In the other copies of the first volume, one also finds sections enclosed in a folder; some of these folders are provided with a number, but none of these numbers has an index.) Considering the way sections in the manuscript that Frau Haas did give to Robert Lammer are numbered, it is most probable: (1) that a second typescript was made; (2) that the sections of this typescript were enclosed in folders numbered:

$$12, 22, 32, \ldots, n2;$$

(3) that this typescript was a copy of the manuscript of the second volume; and
(4) that the disappeared parcel contained this typescript.
40 Karl Popper, *Die beiden Grundprobleme der Erkenntnistheorie* (1979; ²1994), p. 449.
My edition of *Die beiden Grundprobleme* contains all the material that could be found (including a short summary written in the autumn of 1932: *Zusammenfassender Auszug (1932) aus Die beiden Grundprobleme der Erkenntnistheorie*). Popper has added a *Vorwort 1978*, a long *Einleitung 1978*, and many new footnotes (1975-1977); he has also inserted corrections (1975-1977) of the old text. All new material is clearly marked, so that the old text can be easily identified. (Cf. ›Nachwort des Herausgebers‹, 1979.)
41 Karl Popper, *The Logic of Scientific Discovery* (1959; and later editions).
42 Karl Popper, *Logik der Forschung* (1934; 2.-10. Aufl., 1966-1994; 11. Aufl., ed. by Herbert Keuth, *Gesammelte Werke* 3, 2005).
43 Karl Popper, *Die beiden Grundprobleme der Erkenntnistheorie* (1979; ²1994), p. 227.
44 Karl Popper, *op. cit.*, pp. 368 ff., 375 ff., and 398 f.
45 Karl Popper, *op. cit.*, p. 399.
46 Novalis (Friedrich von Hardenberg), *Novalis Schriften* II. (edited by Friedrich Schlegel and Ludwig Tieck, 1802), ›Dialog 5‹ (1798), p. 429. Cf. Karl Popper, *op. cit.*, p. 399. In *The Logic of Scientific Discovery* (1959; and later editions) and in *Logik der Forschung* (²1966; and later editions), the first lines of the fifth *Dialogue* were to be used as a motto; see my ›Nachwort‹, Section 5, to Karl Popper, *Die beiden Grundprobleme der Erkenntnistheorie* (1979; ²1994), pp. 447 f.

The Birth of Karl Popper's
*The Open Society and Its Enemies.**

Hubert Kiesewetter

1. Introduction

In the third century A.D., the Mauritanian grammarian Terentianus Maurus already knew that books have their own fate when, in his work *Carmen heroicum* (Hero Poem), he made a classic "world 3" statement, "Habent sua fata libelli."[1] He did not know and could never have imagined that, over 1500 years later, the fate of the publication of Karl Popper's *The Open Society and Its Enemies* would prove to be a paradigmatic confirmation of his saying. And the fascinating story of the book's publication is almost unknown, for Karl Popper made amazingly little mention of it in his intellectual autobiography.[2] Even Ernst Gombrich was only able to present us with a glimpse of the work's fate when, on the occasion of the fiftieth anniversary of the book's publication, he quoted from his correspondence with Karl Popper in his wonderful lecture on June 12, 1995 at the London School of Economics and Political Science (LSE).[3] Therefore, I hope that in the following chapters I will be able to present a bit of the gripping fascination associated with the birth of this book, as well as the inner and outer battles involved in its publication, which can be gleaned from reading Popper's extensive correspondence. In order to preserve the authenticity of his correspondence, I will often quote directly from the exchange of letters between Popper and his friends.

On June 29, 1943, after spending eight months unsuccessfully trying to find an American publisher for his book, Popper wrote the following to Fritz Hellin about his work, with the notation *"exclusively* for your own information":

"The book is a very bold and challenging book, not so much in its style, but in its content. It attacks some of the greatest authorities of all times; and not only a few of them, such as Plato, Aristotle, Hegel, etc., but in fact a great number which are not named in the table of contents. And it does so with a recklessness which is excusable only in view of the fact that *I consider the destruction of the awe of the Great Names, the Great Intellectual Authorities, one of the necessary pre-requisites of a recuperation of mankind.* It is, of course, *not* an attempt to put anybody else, or myself, in the place of these Great Names. I rather insist that the whole bumptiousness and pretentiousness with which the business of philosophy is glorified, *must disappear.*

This is one of the reasons why it will be difficult to find an authority to recommend it. The established intellectual authorities will not like it, since it fights against the very idea of an established intellectual authority, and since it undermines their glory. It hits against practically everybody, with very few exceptions, foremost among them Bertrand Russell, who is, in my opinion, not so much by any particular of his doctrine, but by his general attitude and lack of bumptiousness, the only really great philosopher of our time; he has something to say ...

Thus my book will not easily find support from those who are 'arrived', nor from those who hope to 'arrive' one day.

Concerning its other characteristics, I may mention that the book is in many respects different from anything I have written or shall write, in so far as it is a very personal book. The range of philosophical topics, which are all treated in an exceedingly simple manner, is wider than in any book I know, with the possible exception of Plato. It treats the philosophy of history and politics, it criticizes the foundations of ethics; it throws a new light on the history of civilization; it contains an entirely new and surprising view of Plato; it treats problems of modern logic; it criticizes leading modern philosophers such as Wittgenstein; it introduces a new and practical view of social methodology. And there are many other objects treated. And it is never superficial. In fact, the analysis is in nearly every case carried to a depth which need not shirk any comparison, although the terminology and the presentation is so simple and unimposing that superficial critics will surely complain about superficiality. Besides, the book is more arresting and more alive and less scholastic than most philosophical books of our time (apart from Russell's). These judgements may appear to you perhaps merely as a typical statement of an author's megalomania. But perhaps the following admission will correct this impression. In spite of all its virtues described, I do *not* hold this book to be the statement of a new great philosophy. I even do not claim that my general philosophical attitude as expressed in this book, is original. On the contrary. It is a direct development of the much abused 19th century philosophy (of its empiricism and 'materialism') and more particularly, it is unoriginal in view of the very similar general attitude of Bertrand Russell. Although I disagree in thousand little things with Russell, and although my main problem and my own method of logical analyses owe nothing to him, the general philosophical attitude of my book is practically identical with his ... The fact that

I clearly and frankly realize that, in its fundamental outlook upon life, philosophy, science, and our possibilities, the book does not offer anything new, may perhaps convince you that my attitude towards the book is free from any touch of megalomania and that my self-flattering description of its great merits may be taken seriously. As to its importance, I am convinced that political science is on the wrong track and that a new orientation may have amazing practical results, and even fairly quickly. And the task of the book is mainly to combat obstacles which stand in the way of this new orientation."[4]

How can one explain why this book, which received worldwide response after its publication and was translated into 26 languages, could not be published for over three years, in spite of intensive efforts in the U.S.A. and England? I would like to tell this adventurous story, one which almost drove Hennie and Karl Popper to despair, in a rather systematic way. It is my hope that, despite some overlapping of content, the fascination which I previously mentioned will be preserved.

2. The Completion of the Manuscript

We know from Karl Popper[5] that it was Hitler's invasion of Austria in March of 1938, a little more than a year after the Poppers had arrived in Christchurch, that moved him to work out his ideas on the political influence of oracular philosophy or, in other words, on the history of historicism.[6] The extremely adverse conditions under which this occurred are almost impossible to imagine in this day and age.[7] Apparently, Popper already intended to write a *Textbook of Logic* at the end of 1937. Rudolf Carnap wrote to him about this plan on December 29, 1937. "I am not aware of such a book and would find it very desirable if one would be written. Hempel told me that Tarski has his doubts as to whether now is the time for such a book, but I believe it would be good if you would write it. It would probably be advisable if you would take into consideration other books so that the works would not compete against but rather supplement each other and could be used one after the other. I believe that this is definitely possible."[8] Popper wrote back on March 7, 1938, five days before German troops invaded his birthplace of Vienna, "I have already written the first forty pages of my "Textbook". It will not collide with any of the books you mentioned."

One can imagine what an enormous shock it was for the Poppers (and this explains the unbelievable intensity, as described below, with which

Karl Popper worked on the manuscript) when, on March 15, 1938, Adolf Hitler proclaimed from the balcony of the Viennese Hofburg before hundreds of thousands of people, "I speak on behalf of the millions of inhabitants of this beautiful German nation, on behalf of the people of the Steiermark, of Lower and Upper Austria, of Kärnten, of Salzburg, of Tirol, and above all in the name of the city of Vienna, when I assure the additional 68 million fellow Germans listening at this moment in our extensive Reich – this nation is German. She has understood and will fulfill her mission. And may her allegiance to the great German national community never be surpassed."[9] Both Hennie und Karl Popper were born and grew up in this city. They completed their studies in Vienna, were married there in 1930, had taught in the Austrian capital, and now, in far-off New Zealand, „half way to the moon"[10], they were forced to witness the destruction of almost everything they had learned to love and appreciate during three decades of their lives. On April 28,1943, Popper wrote to Gombrich: „Until the outbreak of the war, we have tried to help refugees as much as we could although it really came to very little (about 36 permits). When this was no longer possible, I started to write the book, and I have used every minute for writing, thinking all the time of you people in England who were bombed. I felt that the only thing for me to do was to write something which might be useful. I have worked day and night on it."[11]

But what went to make up the extremely adverse conditions to which I referred earlier? A few hints must suffice here, but they should be mentioned nevertheless. Otherwise one might get the impression that Popper was able to pursue his scientific work in Christchurch largely undisturbed, apart from a lack of literature. On October 15, 1942, he reported rather emotionlessly in a letter to Carnap: "You ask me, in your letter, what I am doing. Apart from teaching, and continuing with probability (I have a few results here) as well as with confirmation, I have concentrated mainly on practical problems of the methodology of the social sciences. It is a war effort. One fruit of this is an article *The Poverty of Historicism,* which will appear, I hope, in Mind. Another is a fairly voluminous book which I have just finished. It is an attack on a kind of superstition introduced into the field of social investigation by Plato and further developed by Hegel and Marx. I have written this book because I believe that it contributes to the understanding of fascism and its dangers and throws light on the present crisis."[12] And he wrote to Hayek on December 16, 1943, "My whole book is, if I may say so, an attempt to make the best out of nothing, i.e., out of the (practically non-existent) literature at my disposal!"[13]

On the one hand, the Poppers had to contend with financial crises, but they shared these difficulties almost solely with the Gombrichs, their closest friends. In 1940, they purchased a 20-year-old wooden house in Cashmere, a southern suburb of Christchurch, with a wonderful view over Christchurch and the Canterbury Plains of the Southern Alps, which they paid off in instalments.[14] Hennie Popper wrote, "The climate is as nearly perfect as things in this world can be, very long summers with an abundance of sunshine, as a matter of fact, we have plenty of sun all the year round. The winter is short and disagreeable, at least for people like us who can't afford good fires."[15] And this despite a winter lasting three months at the most, June through August, in which snow rarely fell in Christchurch. In a relatively small, steep, and rocky garden, Hennie grew vegetables – mostly peas, beans, potatoes, carrots, spinach, artichokes, lettuce and tomatoes – from which they fed themselves, from October to May, as long as their stores lasted. "The rest of the year we live chiefly on a carrot and rice diet, for economy's sake. Karl's salary was never adequate and is now less so than ever. Prices have gone up tremendously and as we have long ago given up the so-called 'luxuries' we try now to save on food and fuel. It is a hopeless job, because we have never spent much on either of these two essentials."[16]

How was it that Popper's salary was insufficient to feed even two people adequately? Had he not chosen the position offered in Christchurch *above* the one in Cambridge because he would earn more there?[17] On July 2, 1945, in the context of his acceptance of the position and salary at the LSE, Popper wrote to Gombrich, "I had here nominally 500 N.Z. £ (which officially equals 400 English £) but after deduction of taxes, superannuation and insurance, only 267 N.Z. £ remained of which we had to pay £130 for the house. This left £137, i.e. 2-12-0 weekly for *all* other expenses. Of course, we could not manage."[18] These financial difficulties could be traced back to the publication of *The Open Society* as well. In a June 1943 letter to Fritz Hellin, Popper included a short overview of his financial situation, which read as follows: "I may perhaps inform you (in connection with my continuous remarks that cables are so expensive) of my income in $. I earn $ 32 weekly. Of these, $ 7 are taxes, $ 8 insurance, superannuation, etc; $ 9 rent, rates; $ 2 light etc. This means that about $ 6 per week remain for food, clothing, tram, typing paper (for which I have to pay and which costs a lot since I consume great quantities). The cables cost each (reply paid) at least $ 6, sometimes $ 9. I have sent about 6 cables to Dorian, and the same number to N. Y. (to Papanek, Braunthal, and you). You can imagine that this is simply disastrous."[19] In addition, Popper regularly sent checks to cover postal expenses to all those with whom he was in contact who were helping to get his book published. He added: "*Please write at once when you see that you need more money for cable-expenses etc.* I do not know, and I cannot find out here, how much you have to pay for cables."[20] Ernst Gombrich was the only person who would have preferred to do without this remuneration. On October 1, 1943, he wrote to Karl Popper: "Thank you so much for the enclosed cheque over £ 4 – but really I don't need or want it. So far I have not spent a fraction of the first £ 4 yet on postage and I shall have to dedicate the rest to some Karl Popper foundation for the promotion of intellectual relations between New Zealand and the United Kingdom."[21]

At the close of the semester in October 1944, Popper wrote about his work plans for the holidays. "Apart from that, I want to do some music. We have not been able to afford a piano here; I had a beautiful Boesendorfer in Vienna, and I could not bring myself to buying a very bad piano; besides, even the worst ones cost more than we could afford. So I bought a harmonium for £ 3-10-0; I repaired it, and it is not so bad, but I am getting hungry for a piano."[22] And even when the position at the London School of Economics was almost within reach and Gombrich assured him that a salary of 600 pounds would be sufficient (see page 27), Popper revealed his concerns, writing, "Hayek's remark quoted by you about not worrying about the fact that the minimum salary mentioned is less than that mentioned to me in his letter seems to indicate that *if* they appoint me, they intend to appoint me at the figure mentioned by Hayek to me, i.e. £ 700 [instead of £ 600, H.K.], rising in two biennial increments of £ 50 to £ 800. This, of course, would give me ... the margin of Agha Khan![23] But I am afraid I shall urgently need all this wealth: my debts, although not at all pressing, are continuously increasing, and if I go to London, I shall have to pay for the voyage etc. which will amount to about £ 360 or 400, and I shall be unemployed for about four months; since I can hardly leave during a term, I may have to give notice for June 1st. This means another £ 120 so that I expect to arrive with a new dept of 480-500! I think it will take me some time before I shall be able to enjoy Agha Khan's wealth!"[24]

In addition to his financial difficulties, Popper also faced health problems. This was no wonder in light of his lifestyle, work and nutritional habits. When he began writing his manuscript, Popper was about 35 years old. However, even a healthier and more robust person would have never survived such physical overexploitation over a period of several years without damaging his or her health. Since he stopped his correspondence almost completely during the writing of *The Open Society*, it is only after

1943 that we are able to once again make any concrete statements as to the state of Popper's health. On May 15, 1943, he wrote to Fritz Hellin, "Literally, we have not had one day's vacation for five years. We are both nearly dead, and very depressed about the obscure fate of the manuscript."[25] And in a desperate letter written on June 29, 1943 concerning the delays in his book's publication, Popper wrote to Hellin, "I have spent so much on cables that we cannot pay our debts, I do not dare to eat a meal at the university canteen, and we do not dare to light a fire." On July 22, 1943, in a letter to Ernst Gombrich, whose willingness to advance the book's publication, as we shall see later, seemed to know no limits, Popper wrote, "I cannot tell you how much I owe to your truly friendly and kind letters. In a time of physical exhaustion and deep depression they really saved me from despair."[26]

The continual delays in the publishing of his "war effort", as Popper often called his book, had their negative effects on Popper's physical and psychological state of health as well. In a letter dated October 12, 1943, Popper wrote to Braunthal, "I must apologize for getting irritated, although, God knows, I have ample reasons ... I am too ill, too tired, and too depressed to continue with the same requests for ever."[27] And on March 1, 1944: "I have read in Upton Sinclair's biography that every book he wrote cost him a tooth: an abscess, developed owing to overwork. This book has cost me nine abscesses and nine teeth; all of them during the last months. This is not pleasant, but a true indication of the whole situation."[28] In contrast, the world looked much rosier after Routledge had accepted the book for publication. Popper wrote to Gombrich on April 22, 1944, "I have a terrible cold – one of the worst I have ever had – but I was never before so happy with a cold!"[29] However, this state soon changed. On the 5th of June, he reported to Gombrich, "I am still very unwell, but I hope I passed through the worst about a week ago when I got a taste of the experience of dissolving at all ends at once. I am taking three different tablets in addition to two other drugs which I use only against symptoms. I continued lecturing all the time: I persuaded a reluctant doctor who wanted me to give them up to agree to it. In fact, I cannot give up lecturing without risking some serious repercussions." After Gombrich had received a copy of the book's outline, worked out in great detail, as well as diverse corrections from Popper, he responded, "I am sure you work too much and sleep to little (I do it the other way round). It doesn't 'pay' in the end. Why can't you refuse some lectures??"[30]

It was under these conditions that Karl Popper wrote *The Open Society and Its Enemies*. I would like to quote Hennie Popper once more, for I could not express it any more impressively in my own words: "For the last four years Karl has been working night and day on the book, I have been typing and doing odd jobs in connection with it. There were no holidays, no Sundays, especially not in the last year. When the Japanese were drawing closer and closer, Karl decided that he would try to finish it as quickly as possible so that he could send the manuscript off before connections with the outside world were interrupted. However, it took him till February this year and in the meantime the war in the Pacific has changed to the better and we were not cut off. During term time, Karl can only work at the weekends, but during the summer holidays he worked literally 24 hours a day. For the last three or four months he was in a state of almost complete exhaustion; he hardly went to bed because he could not sleep. Several times I had an awful fright when he suddenly could not see anymore on one eye. But he just sat and wrote it again, and I typed, and typed it again, hundreds of times."[31]

Popper's health did not improve significantly after Routledge had signed the contract agreeing to publish his book. On August 8, 1944, Popper wrote to Gombrich in response to his long-distance diagnosis, "It is probably quite right, but at the same time the doctor found now what proves to be the immediate cause of all evil – an insufficiency of the adrenal cortex. I get adrenalin injections which seem to make a big difference."[32] Afterwards, there was a relatively long period of time before Popper again experienced problems with his health. "I have the worst cold of my life, which means a lot. I am over the crest of the wave, but I still have a cough, a cold in the head, a sore throat, a pain in one of my joints, and a few minor things: but the worst is a splitting headache (I didn't dare to write 'terrific headache', fearing these words may become my last, as it just happened to a poor, great contemporary)."[33] And on June 12, 1945, after he had received the news of his appointment at the London School of Economics, he wrote to Ernst Gombrich, "We were both somewhat frightened, mainly in view of my rather bad health, and especially the silly way in which my corps reacts to bad weather. I am sick of being sick. You will think me a terrible hypochondriac. So do I, but my doctor (a very nice and kind person and an excellent doctor) says that it is unfortunately all true."[34]

3. The Search for a Publisher

Popper had finished the Plato volume in October of 1942. Since there was less of a paper shortage in the USA than in England and the distance by mail was shorter, and because he was convinced that his book would prove to be an important contribution to the work of political reconstruction after the war, Popper hoped to find a publisher in the United States quickly. A. and H. Braunthal, F. Deutsch, F. Hellin, and E. Papanek were all Viennese friends of Popper's who had been fellow members of the "Vereinigung Sozialistischer Mittelschüler" (Union of Socialist High School Students) after World War I, and who were now living in the U.S.A.[35] He wrote to Frederick Dorian (= Fritz Deutsch), "There must be a philosophy (I do not mean a philosophical *system*) behind the reconstruction plans, and I have tried to contribute to it."[36] He sent the manuscript, along with a covering letter, first to the Macmillan Company, 60 Fifth Avenue, New York City. He intended to then send a further copy to Henry Holt & Co. and to Harcourt, Brace & Co, each at three week intervals, after which, however, there would be no spare copies left. Simultaneously, he tried to make contact with the above-mentioned former Viennese friends, hoping that they could be of assistance in the publishing process.[37] Since the search for a publisher in the USA and in England proceeded very differently, I would like to present the two separately, even though it is possible to do so only somewhat superficially.

A. The USA

On October 23, 1942, Karl Popper wrote a letter, apparently to Frederick Dorian, which I would like to quote, for it reflects the optimism existent at the onset of an undertaking which would eventually turn into a nightmare.

"Dear Friend,
  Thank you very much for your letter. It was good to hear from you again, and I am looking forward to having your book. Please excuse that I have not answered the letter sooner – I have been working too hard.
  I have just finished my new book. I know that you think generally much too highly of me and my abilities and I am therefore reluctant in asserting myself that this book is important. I must say, however, that it is so indeed. It is a war effort; a new philosophy of society and politics which, I

believe, contains a great deal that is dearly needed in our time. The title of the book is

False Prophets
Plato – Hegel – Marx.

But the book offers much more than this title promises.

Now I have singled you out, old friend, to help me in the matter of publication. I do not think that I shall have to worry you too much: there won't be much work involved, I hope.

I am sending the typescript directly to several publishers, and I have asked them to communicate with you, if they are interested, and to return the typescript to you, if they are not interested. And I send you a power of attorney, so that you can act on my behalf, and sign the contract for me.

The reason why I am burdening you with such a responsibility is that communications are so very slow at present that it would be quite impracticable for me to correspond with the publishers directly. Another reason is this: Only the first 210 pages of the typescript are ready for print. The rest which I am revising at present will be ready in five or six weeks hence. But the book ought to be published as soon as possible. I have sent it therefore as it is now to the publishers who should be able come to a decision (and to make the contract with you) on the basis of what I have sent them. In this way I hope to save precious time.

I do not expect you to have expenses. I am sending you a number of international reply coupons. I shall also cable to you, reply paid, so that you will have no expenses for cables. Should you have any other expenses please let me know at once: I shall then at once apply for a permit to send you the money. It is, I hear, not so difficult now if it is not a big sum, and if it is to stay in U.S.A.

We are both not very good in matters of correspondence, and I am the worst of us; that is to say, I understand how hard it is to write letters. But I trust that in a matter like the present, this will not play any role. I have been working on this book for four years practically day and night; you will understand how I feel about it.

I do not think that there will be great difficulties in securing a publisher. The book is, as you will see, most readable, and, if anything, rather more topical than I wish it to be. I should like you, however, to write in about two months to those publishers who have not acknowledged to you the receipt of the MS, enquiring whether they have got it.

I include in this letter a copy of the letter I am sending to the publishers. And I am sending by the same mail a copy of the typescript to you; *please keep it carefully*; it may be needed for printing. I should be glad if you would read it, but please, do not show it to anybody, and treat the whole matter as *strictly confidential* towards anybody until the publication of the book.

Please, old F., take great care in this matter. I rely fully on you.

That is, more or less, all. My wishes concerning the contract with the publisher I enclose separately.

I have not heard from Hellin again. I should very much like to know how he and his family is. I am not very well. I am overworked and ill, and I am getting very, very old. But I have a number of important things to write yet. Indeed, if I am dissatisfied with the book then it is because it leaves so much unsaid that is urgent.

Dear F., it was nice of you to ask about me. I am quite well, though the book has left its marks on me too. We both hope to see you again before too long."[38]

On November 18, 1942, Popper had yet to receive an answer confirming that his manuscript and letter had arrived. He sent a power of attorney and a check for $10 and added, among other things, "I do not think that the war will last long; although Churchill says it is only the end of the beginning, it is, I think, the beginning of the end. And when it is all over, we may come to visit you one day." In a letter written on February 8, 1943 and posted on February 16th, Frederick Dorian replied, "It is with great satisfaction that I received so tangible a proof that you are alive, active and at work: Your manuscript is on my desk and the publishers, too, have it and study it."[39]

However, the hope that a publisher for the book would soon be found in the USA was not to be fulfilled. It seemed as though the whole world had conspired against Karl Popper and his work, as if, as Popper wrote to Hellin on June 29, 1943, an "amazing conspiracy of black magic" was at work. First, the slowness of correspondence severely tested Popper's patience. (At the time, letters took 6 to 8 weeks from New Zealand to the USA because it was forbidden to send them by airmail.) And then there was the lack of willingness, in Popper's eyes, on the part of his American friends to read his book and/or his extensive instructions[40] carefully and to send copies of the manuscript, one after the other, to the nine American publishers he had initially selected. Hellin wrote, "Dorian sent me a fortnight ago the manuscript of Karl's book and I shall try my best to have it published here in this country. Alfred Braunthal cabled him a few days ago that I am taking care of this matter as I am perhaps today the one of Karl's friends who has the most opportunity to help him with this matter."[41] In their attempts to find a publisher as soon as possible, Popper's friends, contrary to his instructions, tried to get well-known and influential people (for example, Carl J. Friedrich or Felix Kaufmann) to read the manuscript. Karl Popper saw this as a violation of his rights as an author, especially in light of his strong attacks on Plato, Hegel, Marx and Mannheim. Over and over he stressed in these, or similar, words: *"I do not wish the book to be shown round to anybody with the only exception of publishers. Please, conform strictly with this fundamental wish of mine."*[42] After it became apparent that Fritz Hellin was not capable of fulfilling Popper's high expectations, he turned to Braunthal in order to expedite the book's publication.

On February 23, 1943, Popper sent Frederick Dorian the second and third sections of the book, namely pages 211- 492, as well as important notes on all 25 chapters, a new preface, the table of contents, and the introduction, all of which he called the "Final MS". However, he apparently continued to work uninterrrupted on the manuscript. At the end of March 1943, Macmillan and Harper rejected the publication of the Plato volume without giving a specific reason. The telegram sent to Popper on April 1, 1943, read as follows: "Harpers and Macmillan rejected manuscript as untimely still waiting to [hear] from others affectionately Frederick Dorian."[43] Popper believed "that an apparent aggressiveness against Marxism most likely [was] the cause of the rejections".[44] He called the new revised manuscript, accompanied by new titles for both volumes, the "May-MS". He also sent a copy of this manuscript to the economist John B. Condliffe in Berkley, California, with the comment "that its publication is urgent"[45] and the request that he read it and perhaps, if he liked it, that he recommend it to W. W. Norton, who had published Condliffe's book *The Reconstruction of World Trade.*[46] However, this hope fell through as well, although Condliffe's secretary at the *Carnegie Endowment for International Peace* in New York had written to Popper on July 27, 1943, "He also had an interview several days ago with Dr. Braunthal to whom he gave your manuscript for reading. After Dr. Braunthal has read the manuscript he will get in touch again with Dr. Condliffe and they will discuss what steps should be taken in regard to trying to interest a publisher in it." Popper was rather dejected about this development and wrote to Hellin, "I have got the feeling that the affair has got completely out of hand, and I do not see why this should be so."[47] Apparently he was right, for a few days later, on May 22, Hellin wrote, "We have all agreed [i.e. he, Dorian, and Braunthal, H.K.] that there is very little chance now for publishing a book like yours", and he suggested to Popper that he "accept the fact that changes in style, cutting and the toning down of ideas will also have to be made. For example, it is more than questionable if a publisher will tolerate the tone of your criticism of Aristotle."

The uncertainty about how things should proceed increased, and Popper, of course, had absolutely no insight into the world of American publishing. He went on to put together a list of 22 American publishers and their respective addresses,[48] "ordered according to desirability", who, one after the other, should receive a letter and a copy of the manuscript.[49] Popper, however, was unsure as to whether the manuscript should be sent to several publishers simultaneously, and whether all or only a portion of the notes should be included, but he did write, "It is of course necessary to send a stamped reply-envelope with the letter, as well as stamps for returning the MS by registered mail."[50] Nevertheless, the combined efforts of Frederick Dorian, Fritz Hellin, and finally Alfred Braunthal failed to lead to any tangible result. Although Dorian wrote, "believe me, these friends of yours are doing everything possible for the book, but of course the book has to stand on its own merits and the New York publishers are a hard-boiled lot"[51], no publisher accepted the book for publication.

Alfred Braunthal appeared to be the person who could rescue Popper out of this publishing misery. He was not only a social philosopher, but had also invited Popper to a lecture on historicism at his house in Brussels in February of 1936, where the two had discussed the topic.[52] Popper wrote, "I had had always only you in mind, since I knew from our talks in Brussels how much you were interested in the problems treated in the book."[53] Since Braunthal had moved several times within the USA, however, Popper's cables did not reach him. It was not until May 19, 1943 that Popper received Braunthal's correct address, as well as Hellin's, from Ernest Papanek.[54] Two days later, Popper wrote to Hellin, who had received the manuscript from Dorian, "Please give Braunthal the MS to read. I do not ask you to read it – it would probably bore you to tears. But I want *one* man over there to know the book and to act on its behalf rather than on my behalf."[55] On the same day he wrote a long letter to Hilde and Alfred Braunthal, in which he explained why he had not reached them by mail despite repeated efforts. "It is the distance, and the time it takes before a letter arrives, and before one knows whether one's letter has reached its destination; all this is so disheartening. And the feeling that long before the letter arrives, things might have completely changed. And apart from that, there was nothing to say. After the fall of France, the war was too dreadful to write about. It is different now, with victory not far away. But even now I find very little to tell you about ourselves: we do nothing but work, I writing, Henny typing. All our interests are confined to this work, which is our war effort; and by sending you a part of its results, I tell you more about us than I could say in a hundred letters."[56]

After Braunthal had received the May-Manuscript (Hellin confirmed this in a July 13, 1943 telegram), Popper hoped that it would be sent to the publishers he had mentioned on an ongoing basis. Braunthal, however, was unable to hold out any significant hopes for Popper, although after reading the manuscript he wrote, "So deeply was I moved by your writing, so excited was I and even thrilled that I devoured the entire book as it were in one gulp."[57] After speaking with Condliffe in New York, who wa not of the opinion that "commercial publishers [would] be able to do anything" about the book's publication, but rather recommended to have the book published by a university press, Braunthal wrote, "The trouble with these publishers is that they require authors to share in the costs. This would mean 500 – 700 (?) dollars costs for the author. Condliffe remarked that even if you had got this money, you would not be permitted to transfer it to this country."[58] Apart from the fact that Popper did not have that kind of money at his disposal, the idea of also having to *pay* for the publication of his book, after all his efforts and hardships, was unacceptable to him. On August 23, 1943, he responded to Braunthal, "Regarding my worries with the book, I have now practically given up hope, at least as far as the U.S.A. are concerned. I am determined not to pay a penny towards publication costs; it is against my principles to buy the privilege of being printed, and I do not think that I should consider it even if I had the money."[59] With this, the issue of an American publication of the book was not closed, but put on ice for the time being. In other words, it was only pursued by Popper half-heartedly. Braunthal still attempted to get the book published by John Day Publishers and afterwards by Yale University Press, in both cases without success.[60] As late as March 19, 1944, Braunthal wrote to Popper, "Karl, we must face the fact that it is extremely hard to get a publisher for a book that is substantially over 100,000 words, and the trouble with a two-volume edition is not only that publishers are extremely hesitant to take this risk, but that the manuscript is so divided that the first volume would, in the eyes of the publisher and of the general reading public, be of less topical interest than the second."[61] And such was the case, for two months later Braunthal wrote, "...the N.C. University Press did not give us the opportunity of a choice. They sent the manuscript back, in a very brusque and tactless way, that is to say, without any explanation."[62] It was not until 1950 that the American edition of *The Open Society* was brought out by Princeton University Press.

In the meantime, Popper had made contacts in England with Ernst H. Gombrich and Friedrich A. von Hayek, writing, "In view of the fact that I have made no progress with this matter since October last year, I have decided to attempt to place the book in England, in spite of the greater paper shortage there."[63] While he had little hope, after all he had gone through, "that anything [would] emerge from such an attempt", his friend Gombrich would do all he could in his power to help.

B. England

It is necessary for us to go back in time several months in order to understand why Popper believed he would now have a better chance of getting his book published in England than in the U.S.A. There had been a short exchange of letters between the Poppers and the Gombrichs at the end of 1937 and during 1938, but while writing his book, Karl Popper had apparently no longer answered Ernst Gombrich's letters.[64] On April 12, 1943, Gombrich sent a telegram to Popper reading, "New Address PO Box 60 Reading kind thoughts", to which Popper replied by cable on April 14th, "Need your help finding publisher book on social philosophy reconstruction problems may I send manuscripts affectionately Popper."[65] On April 16th, Popper wrote the following letter:

"Dear Ernst, I have not heard from you for a long time and I was very glad to get your cable. I very much hope that all is well with you and your family. The reason why you have not heard from us is that I have been writing a book. The manuscript is finished; its title is 'A Social Philosophy for Everyman'. (It has about 700 pages i.e. about 280.000 words.) I believe that the book is topical and its publication urgent – if one can say such a thing at a time when only one thing is really important, the winning of the war. The book is a new philosophy of politics and of history, and an examination of the principles of democratic reconstruction. It also tries to contribute to an understanding of the totalitarian revolt against civilization, and to show that this is as old as our democratic civilization itself. – The day before yesterday I sent you a cable to PO Box 60, Reading, asking for your help in this matter. You are the only dependable friend I have in England. In view of the immense postal and other difficulties it is absolutely impossible to send the book from here to a publisher and have it sent back if it is rejected; for that would mean anything up to one year's delay in case of one rejection. This is why I need somebody in England who sends the MS to the various publishers. I should be very grateful if you would be prepared to undertake this. In my cable I asked you to do this for me; but I am sending this letter for your further information without waiting for your reply. I know that I am asking a lot of you, but I do not know of any other possibility, and I hope that it won't mean very much work for you, *only writing a few letters*. When I have your consent, I shall apply here for a permit to send you some money to cover your postal expenses. With many thanks and kindest regards,

Yours ever, K."[66]

Gombrich telegraphed on April 24, 1943, "Looking forward seeing manuscript shall naturally do my best." This was not only the actual beginning of a lifelong friendship, but also marked the onset of an incredibly extensive correspondence from April, 1943 to November, 1945, culminating in the publication of *The Open Society and Its Enemies* and Popper's immigration to England. Gombrich did not merely write "a few letters", but sacrificed almost all of his spare time in order to find a publisher for the book, despite his being under great pressure himself in his job with the English Secret Service.[67] An ironic twist in the fate of the book's publication can be found in reading Popper's letter to Gombrich dated May 4, 1943, where he asks him to "Please make the following change: relegate Kegan Paul-Routledge to a later place, perhaps after Faber; the reason is this: the attitude of my book is diametrically opposed to that of K. Mannheim and criticizes him; but Mannheim is editor of one of Kegan Paul's International Libraries (of Sociology and Social Reconstruction). Therefore if you approach Kegan Paul-Routledge, you would have to tell them that my book contains a criticism of Mannheim which I should prefer Mannheim not to see before publication".[68] After an almost endless odyssee, of which I would only like to share the most important segments, *The Open Society* was eventually published by none other than George Routledge & Sons.

One initial difficulty was that Gombrich had no direct connections with a publisher or publishing house and was no longer at the Warburg Institute in London. However, he did have colleagues who knew Popper and who were willing to establish such contacts, such as Ilse Pollak and Lux Furtmueller. Seven days after the above-mentioned letter, he wrote to Popper, "Have you any 'bigwigs' here whom you could mention as reference? I know that Mannheim is now publishing a series of books on social philosophy, would that be a possible candidate?"[69] As a result, Popper wrote letters to Prof. L. Susan Stebbing[70] and Prof. Friedrich A. von Hayek,[71] who, in turn, corresponded with Gombrich. Stebbing wrote, "I have received Dr. P's letter. I should be ready to read the typescript and help if I can. I am at present ill in bed and I do not know how I shall be but if you care to send it in spite of the fact that I might not be well enough to read it when it came, please do." In a letter from Hayek we read, " ... if I can in any way help in trying to place the MS with a publisher I shall be very glad to do what I can. It so happens that I have just finished myself a book on rather similar problems and I doubt whether the publishers of the book (Routledges) would be prepared to take another similar book, at any rate till the first has come out. But I have several other publishing connections which might be of use ..."[72] Gombrich favored giving Prof. Stebbing priority.[73]

On July 10, 1943, Gombrich received Popper's first manuscript, which had been mailed on April 29th. He responded by telegram, "Manuscript arrived safely" – though the name of the telegram's recipient mistakenly read Potter instead of Popper![74] Gombrich began reading the manuscript immediately and a day later wrote, "I have started reading it last night and this morning and have reached page 50 or so – so far I am fascinated both by the lucidity of arguments and by the interest of the subject matter ... I can also imagine what amount of care and labour your wife must have invested in the typing and packing. It looks 'wie aus dem Schachterl' [particularly accurate and well done]."[75] At the same time, he attempted to introduce the book to several publishing houses, with the assistance of influential scientists. On July 12, 1943, Hayek had written to Popper, "When the manuscript arrives I shall be very glad to help Dr. Gombrich, so far as is in my power, to get it published. It is not quite easy nowadays, but I have little doubt we shall succeed."[76] At the end of July, Gombrich telegraphed Popper, "Hayek strongly advises seizing concrete Cambridge Press chance. Myself doubt deterrent effect but less salesmanship likely. Please cable views", and wrote afterwards in a letter, "You must wonder at the many telegrams I sent you about Hayek and the Cambridge Press. The point is that he knows the philosopher of the board who would have to recommend it"[77] However, even if Cambridge Press were to accept the manuscript, Hayek believed its publication would take about a year.[78] In a letter to Gombrich, Hayek continued, "I fear even that with an ordinary publisher we should have great difficulties to place it at all on account of its length and paper difficulties, even if we have the luck of finding a publisher whose reader properly appreciates the rare quality of the book." On

August 12, 1943, after receiving a cable from Popper giving his approval, Gombrich sent the manuscript to Cambridge Press, where the board planned to make its decision on the book's acceptance on September 24th. At the same time, Gombrich expressed his fears, writing, "that printing and especially binding takes a very long time now not so much because of shortage of material but because of shortage of labour".[79] We shall see just how right he was.

Popper replied, "I need not repeat how glad I would be if the Cambridge Press would accept the book; I am naturally somewhat disappointed to hear that publication would take a year or so; and I wonder whether they might possibly be prepared (*after* acceptance) to arrange with their likely agents in U.S.A., the Oxford Press New York, for publication there as early as possible: I gather it is rather usual to have books set up in U.S.A., where they must be set up if the Copyright is to be secured, and the plates sent to England."[80] He requested – adding "I should not dream of making it a condition" – that both publications should be carried out as soon as possible. However, on October 25th, Gombrich had to telegraph Popper the news, "Unfortunately Cambridge disappointed Levy trying Nelson". On October 13th, Gombrich had already written that Hayek had informed him that Cambridge Press "do not officially give any reasons in such cases but I have been told in strict confidence ... that the two decisive reasons after very careful discussion and on the basis of a very detailed report were the length of the book and, the second point is a little comic, that as a University Press they ought not to publish a book which is so disrespectful of Plato".[81] Due to the increasing shortage of paper and because publishers were concentrating on books that would have a "very rapid turnover", Hayek was not very optimistic that the book could be published very soon. As a possible next step, he suggested to write to the publishers Allen and Unwin or Jonathan Cape. He also mentioned his connections with Macmillan and Routledge, but added his concern "that in the case of Routledge he knows from his own experience how difficult and slow everything has become!" In addition to the mathematician Hyman Levy, Esther Simpson, secretary of the *Society for the Protection of Science and Learning,* was willing to lend her support to get the book published.

The publishing house Macmillan seemed to be the most promising in Popper's eyes for two reasons. First of all, Hayek might be able to influence his colleagues A.L. Bowley and A.Wolf at the London School of Economics, who were the editors of LSE's *Studies in Statistics and Scientific Method,* published by Macmillan. Secondly, B.P. Wiesner also knew this publishing company and could recommend the book. Nevertheless, on November 13, 1943, Popper suggested to Gombrich that he ought to approach perhaps two publishers simultaneously. "I think it is only fair to do that, considering the time they take. I hope you won't get impatient even if matters continue to get from bad to worse." Gombrich didn't agree with this plan, however, because, Laski had read the manuscript on behalf of Nelson and was enthusiastic. He wrote, "Hayek is very glad about that and so am I because, although Nelson's are not bound to accept his recommendations, Laski's prestige in intellectual circles here is very great and I have little doubt that a book about which he is enthusiastic will get published. Unfortunately I cannot agree with your suggestion in your wire to try other publishers simultaneously."[82] Popper countered with the following proposal: "You have not tried Unwin yet, nor Macmillan, Gollancz, Cape, Secker. I suggest the following procedure: if Nelson's rejection has not yet come, write to Levy and ask him to propose a reasonable time-limit (say another three weeks) after which he would consider you free from obligation not to submit the book to anybody else ... And as soon as this period is over, I suggest to approach simultaneously some of the firms mentioned above".[83]

Although 1943 was slowly coming to a close, the odyssee was still not over. "[In] view of Hayek's great and warm interest", however, Popper suggested to Gombrich that he cooperate closely with Hayek in considering what additional steps could be taken. On December 4th he wrote, "The best would be to get Hayek or somebody who is enthusiastic *and* a bigwig to see the next publisher eg Unwin personally ... and to extract promise of early decision and, if possible, that he reads parts of the book himself."[84] On December 13th, Popper made a concrete proposal. "I wonder whether anybody within your or Hayek's reach knows Sir Alfred Zimmern of Oxford. If he were ready to read the book, then this may open the way to Oxford University Press."[85] In early 1944, however, Popper had to bear yet another setback when he received a telegram from Gombrich reading, "Nelson regrets no paper wish better news 1944."[86] There is an amusing story behind the arrival of this telegram, whose sender and recipient had apparently been switched. Popper writes, "To-day I was in the College (we have vacations now), and by the purest accident, I was asked by the Rector's secretary whether I happen to know some person named Conbrick (sic!). On my ardent protestation that I do, I was told that a week ago, a telegram had been delivered to the College, addressed to Ernest Conbrick, University, Ch., but was not accepted since this person was unknown to the College." After Nelson's rejection, Popper had become uncertain which publisher might be the right one. "I have heard much of Unwin's outstanding personality and initiative. On the other hand, Macmillan may be able to settle the U.S.A. business with one stroke ... I have the feeling that Unwin might (if Laski urges him) decide more quickly. Speed, of course, is now my main concern, and if Cape (of whom Hayek wrote that he has paper) or anybody else should offer prospects of a speedy decision, then he should be approached next."[87]

On January 16, 1944, Ernst Gombrich wrote Popper, "Yesterday I got this very nice letter from Hayek. He writes that we may still hope to find something better than Nelsons. That he had a talk with Mr Stanley Unwin some time ago who said that 'while he would probably accept the book it would be with no commitment as regards the date of publication and with a mental reservation to keep it indefinitely till the paper situation improves. I don't feel we ought to risk this.' (Nor do I) Hayek goes on: 'My inclination would be to try Macmillan next. With the [only] exception of the two great University Presses they are undoubtedly the best and I have a special reason to suggest them now. My copy of the typescript has ... just been read by my friend Professor Lionel Robbins, who thinks as highly of it as I do, and he has a certain amount of influence with Macmillans. I think that, if you wish him to do so, he would even be prepared [himself] to submit it to them with his recommendation ...' Hayek concludes that he has no opinion whether it would be expedient to approach several publishers at the same time but in the case of Macmillan he should prefer that no other attempt is made at that time. 'But should we fail [there] again perhaps we should really do it, perhaps in the form that you approach one and I another publisher'."[88] On February 7th, however, Gombrich complained a bit about Hayek, writing, "I don't think it was quite right of him to listen to Robbins and to go straight to Kegan without even so much as asking me. Nevertheless one must be 'grateful', which is sometimes a little burdensome."[89]

In March 1944, with still no possibility of publication in sight, Popper made the following suggestion to Hayek: "I should of course very much prefer to have the whole thing published rather than only the Plato part, or at least, the second volume accepted for later publication; but I should agree to the publication of Plato only."[90] A month later, all of this had been forgotten – on April 10, 1944, Gombrich telegraphed: "Routledge Contract British Empire rights publication within 12 months two volumes not exceeding Guinea each stop first 2000 ten percent royalties then 15 advance £ 50."[91] On the same day, Popper replied in a letter expressing his deep joy. "I need not tell you what it means to us. I was very near to giving up all hopes. We are very happy, though we hardly dare to trust fate yet, and feel that we ought not to be happy in a time like this. But it is amazing how one's outlook on life can change in a few minutes. – Ernst, I cannot tell you how wonderful you have been in this trying time, and how profoundly grateful we are."[92] The search for a publisher, which had lasted a year and a half, had thus come to an end. The subsequent difficulties in Routledge's publication of the book will be illustrated in a later section.

4. The Search for a Title

From the start, Karl Popper was convinced that finding an attractive title (and subtitle) for his book would necessarily play a decisive role in securing a publisher during the war, as well as in assuring the book's subsequent sales success. (I am not referring here to the diverse changes in the chapter titles and their content.) He wrote to Braunthal, "I have some experience with publishers, and I think that the title question is important for placing the book."[93] As a result, the search for the right title remained a central theme throughout all of Popper's correspondence. It is for this reason that I would like to devote a few thoughts to the subject. We have already heard that the book's initial title was meant to be *False Prophets: Plato-Hegel-Marx*. Popper searched for a better title even before the book's rejection by Macmillan, although this proved to motivate his search all the more. He wrote to Hellin, "The old title was brisk and informative, but unfortunately, the information it conveyed was misleading, and it must therefore be dropped. It will be better not to mention Marx in the title at all, in order not to irritate the publishers; at least, until after the book is accepted."[94] The new title, *A Critique of Political Philosophy,* although less provoking, was "a bit heavy", and therefore not completely satisfactory either. On May 21, 1943, Popper wrote to Braunthal, "... I have not got a really good new title." As possible alternatives, depending upon which publisher was being approached, Popper suggested *A Social Philosophy For Everyman* or *A Social Philosophy For Our Time.*

The question of a title, however, continued to haunt Popper. We read, "Again the title-question The 'Critique'-title ran originally like this: 'From Plato to Marx – A Critique of Political Philosophy'. In this form, the title is much better, alluding as it does to 'Capital – A Critique of Political Economy' ... But I am afraid to mention Marx in the title now."[95] After Harper had also refused to publish the book, Popper wrote to Fritz Hellin in a letter dated May 15, 1943, "*This is not the time of an anti-Marx book.*"[96] Hellin did little in the way of dispelling Popper's worries and encouraging him, writing shortly thereafter, "You need not worry about the title. No American publisher would accept such an abstract title as you have given. Such things, if you really want the book published, must be left to the judgement of the publishers with their long years of experience in such matters."[97] Afterwards, Popper wrote to Braunthal on July 20, 1943, "Prof. Carnap whom I have told about its content, strongly suggests in a letter that it may be the old title which might prevent publishers from even considering it. Please, see that any trace of the old title is eradicated before the MS is sent to any further publisher, and also that the new 'Title Parts' replace the old ones."[98]

Similarly, the issue of a fitting title came up repeatedly in Popper's correspondence with Gombrich and Hayek. In a letter to Gombrich on October 11, 1943, Popper added the handwritten comment, "Could you write to me about the title problem more fully?"[99], which Gombrich did in his reply dated November 15th. "I have thought a lot about the title question but I am inclined to think that your 'From Plato to Marx, a Critique ...' is really the best. If it were possible to condense a title somewhat like the following into a much briefer formula it would perhaps characterise the book even better: "The dangerous heritage of Historicism – a contribution towards a philosophy of Democracy" or "Dangerous Legacy – A Critical Analysis of Social Thought from Plato to Marx". Or even more 'propagandist' "The Fetish of History – A plea for a democratic philosophy." You see, what I would like to see is the "challenge" character of the book expressed in the title – as you had it in the "Three False Prophets" which, however, seems to me not to do the book full justice because it lays too much stress on the negative aspect of the book while I should like to find a title which expresses both the polemical and the positive side (the Critique title is right for the 'educated' readers but it *might* look rather formidable for others whom you ought to reach.) "The Worship of History as a challenge to rational social thought", something on these lines might perhaps convey some of it but it all is too long and heavy. What about: "From Plato to Marx – a Critical Analysis of anti-democratic thought"? – Further to the chapter Headings: If you would agree to consider the principle suggested on the previous airgraph page you might perhaps take the names into the titles of the three Parts that is: "The Open Society and its first Antagonists: Heraclitus and Plato" [;] "The Rise of Oracular Philosophy: From Aristotle to Hegel" [;] "The High Tide of Prophecy: Marx and after". All these are, of course, very unimportant suggestions. If you have no time please don't bother to reply to them."[100]

On October 26, 1943, Popper wrote to Hayek, "You are only too right in your criticism of my title and the table of contents ... The title question has troubled me for a long time. My first title was perhaps the best, but I dropped it because it was open to misinterpretation. It was: False Prophets (Plato-Hegel-Marx). (I dropped it mainly because Marx, as opposed to Plato, is not so much a wolf in a sheep's hide, but rather a sheep in a wolf's hide – a puritan moralist posing as an immoralist.) I like your title 'The Conflict of Political Ideals', but it may also be somewhat misleading: it may mislead the reader to expect that I deal with the conflict between my main heroes, Plato, Hegel, and Marx, while, in fact, it alludes to *my* conflict with all of them! What do you say to (1) 'The Open Society And Its Enemies', (2) 'A Social Philosophy For Everyman' (or, if it is not too pretentious, For Our Time), (3) The Flight From Freedom (or From the Open Society). I nearly despair of finding a really good title!"[101]

It wasn't until December 4th that Hayek responded, saying, "I do not think the 'Open Society' should appear in the title: it does not immediately convey the meaning it assumes in the book. The Flight from Freedom would be good if a book with an almost identical title had not recently appeared. 'A Social Philosophy for Everyman' (or 'for our Time') is a little too neutral, but may be relatively the best. Personally I still like the Conflict of Political (or Social) Ideals better but it is far from ideal." And on January 29, 1944, he continued, "I am not yet happy about the title. I don't think that any title which begins simply with 'A Social Philosophy', whether it be 'for To-Day', 'for Everyman', or 'for Our Time', is really effective. But 'An Introduction to Social Philosophy' might well form an explanatory subtitle to some other more striking main title. 'The Open Society and its Enemies' is better than the others, but the unfamiliarity of the phrase 'open society' is a serious drawback; but it has the advantage of an 'and' in it, which usually makes a good title. It is now unfortunately almost imperative to avoid the word freedom in the title, so much nonsense has it had to cover in recent years. 'The Conflict of Political Ideals' which I suggested before, is by no means ideal. Perhaps 'The Perennial Contest of Ideals', with subtitle as above, is better? All this is merely to suggest that you ought to keep this important question turning [over] in your mind in the hope that the right title will still present itself."

It was the friendly modesty of Ernst Gombrich – and perhaps also T. Murray Ragg – which apparently led to others receiving the laurels for suggesting or discovering the final title of *The Open Society*.[102] On March 14, 1944, Popper wrote to Gombrich, "I think you are right that the best compromise possible is to publish Plato with Notes separately (as I considered during the writing of the book). It is quite self contained. Title: The Open Society and Its Enemies. If the second volume is published, it would have the same title, with the sub-title: vol. II, The Rise of Oracular Philosophy."[103] After a conversation between Gombrich, Hayek, and Herbert Read in the London Reform Club, the title *The Open Society and Its Antagonists. Volume I: The Age of Plato; Volume II: The High Tide of Prophecy* was favored.[104] Popper responded in a letter dated April 14, 1944, "I do not mind whether the title is 'The Open Society and Its Enemies' or 'The Open Society and its Antagonists'. Prof. Findlay of Dunedin whose taste I value, strongly recommends the first, saying that it sounds ever so much better. Please, let Mr Read (whose title 'To Hell with Culture' is so outstanding) decide this aesthetic question. I am equally satisfied with both versions."[105] However, eight days later he had come to a different conclusion: "I strongly recommend THE OPEN SOCIETY AND ITS ENEMIES rather than 'And Its Antagonists'. Reasons: The 'Antagonists' were suggested by me at a time when it was the title neither of the whole book nor of vol. I, but merely of part I. I preferred them because of the subtle shade of meaning (they imply a kind of natural counter-action against the open society, rather than blind enemy)."[106]

With this, however, the question of a title had still not been put to rest, for on June 5, 1944, Popper wrote to Gombrich, "You will remember that the original title of the book was *'False Prophets'* with the sub-title 'Plato-Hegel-Marx'. The reaction of some people towards this title made me suggest to drop it, at least until the book is accepted by some publisher. On the other hand, I am still inclined to think that it is the best title of all, and I wanted it at least *considered* by the publisher. I suppose it has been considered and rejected; if so, then everything is in order, and I am quite satisfied that *The Open Society and Its Enemies* is the second best of all titles so far discussed. But I do not *know* whether the 'False Prophets' have ever been considered. It is this matter where I feel rather uncertain, and where I should not like to have the final decision myself; for so much depends on the 'local' situation, as it were, on some estimate of the reaction of the public ... If, however, you want to know which title I should prefer if I had not to consider anything else, then I must say that it would be my original title. It avoids, apart from other things, the difficulties of the historical incompleteness of the book."[107] A few days later, on June 10th, Gombrich wrote to Popper, "This is just quickly to tell you that Routledges Managing Director (Mr. T. Murray Ragg) wrote to me 'we are all agreed here that The Open Society and its Enemies is much preferable to ... its antagonists. We entirely agree also that The Spell of Plato is better then the Age ...'."[108] And this eventually turned out to be the final title and subtitle of the first volume, while the subtitle *The High Tide of Prophecy: Hegel, Marx and the Aftermath* was accepted for volume two.

5. States of Despair

We have already heard that Popper and his wife had worked for years with incredible intensity on the completion of the book. All the greater must have been their disappointment when the intensive efforts to publish the book in the U.S.A. and England repeatedly failed. Several times Popper was on the edge of despair and had lost all hope that a publisher for *The Open Society* would ever be found. I would like to quote several passages from Popper's letters which reveal, subjectively and objectively, just how desparate his situation was. This appears important to me in order to refute Malachi H. Hacohen's psychological theses that Popper's life was one of homelessness, social isolation, and estrangement, that he lived in permanent exile, something I believe to be far from the truth.[109] From a rational standpoint, there cannot be the slightest doubt that, upon his being offered the position at the LSE, Popper's great longing was to go to England and establish his home there. When asked by Rudolf Carnap if he would like to return to Vienna or Austria, Popper only answer was, "No, never!"[110] And also Hennie Popper, who would have preferred to have stayed in New Zealand, wrote to Ernst and Ilse Gombrich, most likely at the beginning of September 1945, "Karl is very tired. However, he has now decided to go to England under all circumstances and we hope to arrive there not later than December or January."[111]

On July 20, 1943, Popper wrote to Fritz Hellin:

"Dear Friend,

I received your cable: 'February Manuscript with Friedrich. May Manuscript with Braunthal. Be patient. Await letters.' on July 18th. I cannot tell you how relieved I was. It was the first confirmation I ever received that any one of the revised manuscripts (February and May) has arrived. I had every reason to worry about it, for I see now from a letter from Dorian I got to-day that at least two letters you wrote to me (and some of Dorian's) must have gone astray. But if so many letters from there get lost, my MSS also might have been lost.

Dorian indicates that when confiding the MSS into your charge, which must have been in April, he wrote together with you a combined letter, and that you and he also wrote separately. I never received any of these letters. I have so far not received anything from you directly, apart from the above quoted cable. I wonder whether this cable was a reply to my cable sent more than a month ago inquiring after the February MS, or a reply to my letters of May 21st and June 3rd?

I hope that I shall soon get a letter from you which will put me entirely at ease. If you *say* that you will do what I have asked for, i.e. send the MS round to the various publishers, and not show it to anybody else without my authority, then I shall be as happy as can be. You say: 'Be patient.' Please, trust me that I shall be as patient as Knight Toggenburg. I fully realize that I cannot expect quick results in a publication issue; that it may take many months before a publisher is found who is interested. Please, believe me, I shall never worry you or press you to achieve results, for I know that it is not in your power to produce them at will. – I have very little hope that the book will be published on the force of recommendations (such as by Friedrich or Condliffe). Only the sending round to publishers will do, and that takes time, and I am clear that nobody can assure success. – I was never impatient in this respect; I only wanted to be informed. I wanted to know whether a manuscript on which I was working terribly hard for more than four years, posted in February, had arrived. Nobody can speak about my impatience if you consider that I had to wait until July 18th to hear that it has arrived! ...

I am writing one week after the landing in Sicily, and after the Russians have turned to the offensive. There is much hope now that the war will end soon ..."[112]

However, neither of these hopes were to be realized soon. On October 12, 1943, Popper wrote to Hellin again:

"Dear Friend,

It is now the anniversary of my sending the manuscript to U.S.A., and five months since I got your address, and since I sent you

(1) the MS
(2) a letter with instructions in duplicate
(3) a cheque of $ 10.

I have been waiting patiently for a reply to these. I have written to you again, in June and in July; my last letter was a reply to your cable in which you admonish me to be patient. After this, I did not write but waited patiently, since you told me in your cable to await letters.

Now I think that, as a business man, you will agree that if one waits for a reply in a important matter, one has to give oneself a time-limit. My time-limit was very generous indeed.

I put my case to you plainly. I cannot go on forever waiting for a reply. On the other hand, I do not wish to pester you, especially since you have admonished me to be patient. In view of this, and of the fact that cooperation with you has proved impossible, I have no other choice but to ask you to withdraw from the whole matter, and to turn over everything to Alfred Braunthal ...

I very much regret that I have to write this letter. I am fully convinced you meant well, and that you have done your best in this matter; but either you have not read my letters and instructions, or you have deliberately neglected my only too clearly expressed wishes, though with the best intentions ...

With this, I suggest to drop this whole matter completely; 'let us talk of something else' or, as Beethoven says: 'O friends, not *these* tunes! Let us sing others, and more joyous ones!' ..."[113]

When Alfred Braunthal wrote on August 24, 1943, requesting that substantial cuts be made on all sections of the book (again, I can not go into details here) in order for it to have any chance of being published, and that Popper give him "plein pouvoir to negotiate about cuts and certain 'diplomatic' changes", Popper's reply was decidedly uncompromising: "Your letter has disturbed me so much because you do not seem to realize how difficult, how impossible it is for anybody but myself to change anything without destroying the whole. Never could I give anybody in the world full powers to alter and change the book. Not a sentence must be altered without my consent.

I must say that I do not understand the situation. I send a book to my friends, a good book, you agree, apparently better than you expected. I ask them to act as my agents, to approach publishers, make them read it, if possible without too much delay, for the book has something urgent to say, and finally fight it out with the publisher that I am not ready to accept cuts. And I find, first, that my friends, who have the best opinion of myself, are convinced, before they have opened the book, that it is not sufficiently good [to be] published without me paying the costs. And that when they read it and find to their surprise that I am not writing in order to be published but because I have really something urgent to say, then they do not now decide to act boldly and confidently as my agents, but rather as a fictitious publisher's agent; instead of waiting for a publisher to demand cuts, and fighting these demands in the interest of a valuable book as well as on behalf of the author who knows what he is doing, they themselves suggest these cuts; and then they even anticipate, and act on the assumption, that I shall agree, in spite of my clear statement to the contrary."[114]

These disappointments continued to linger on and were reflected in Popper's correspondence with Gombrich, when he wrote to him about the same time, "Do not believe that I expect *results* from you. (Or from anybody else.) I know very well that the prospects of publishing the book are not good. But I am sure of one thing. If you do not find a publisher, it will not be your fault."[115] After Cambridge Press had rejected the book, Popper wrote, "Sad news, indeed, and I am very sorry to cause you such trouble and disappointment. It opens up a host of problems. Since you do not mention Unwin, I am afraid that, in accordance with your plans you mentioned before, you have already tried him in vain. Also, since you only mention Levy, I am afraid that the Cambridge report was so bad that Hayek does not wish to proceed in the matter; although I most sincerely hope that things are not quite as black as that. I don't like Nelson much, but under the circumstances, I should of course accept; still, I am anxious that Unwin and Macmillan and even Gollancz (and Longmans who is not on my list) should be tried as well, since I should prefer them."[116] And although Popper wrote to Gombrich on November 22, 1943, "...*please*, do not give up hope, even if four or five more rejections should lie ahead!", on November 30th we read, "Much as I try to persuade myself rationally that I cannot do anything to further your attempts, I cannot help racking my brains about it; I feel that it is important that the book is published *before* 'normal' conditions are re-established, since its contribution is of significance for the way in which they should be established ... I am fighting against the depressing feeling that even if I wrote as well as Horace, nobody would print it."[117] Two days before Christmas 1943, Popper complained to his friend, "I have nothing new to report, apart from the fact that I, ungrateful soul that I am, am still very depressed. I fear that the book will not be printed and that I won't get the post."[118] Gombrich proved to be not only more sober, but apparently more far-sighted in his judgment, when answering on January 12, 1944, "As to the possible influence of your book I am more and less optimistic than you. I think it is a kind of book which is less likely to influence the people who are now busy in responsible positions (simply because they don't read and take in any more) but which may have a very substantial long term effect on people who still have a formative mind."[119]

In an act of extreme exertion ("I have not slept at all"), Popper made extensive corrections to volume two, after which he wrote to Gombrich, "It was a colossal job here and I was (and am) very ill while doing it. The doctor had strictly forbidden any work, and I am, of course, now absolutely down again."[120] In March 1945, upon hearing from Gombrich that Hayek had not been present at the decisive meeting concerning the position at the LSE, he was once again plunged into a state of despair. He writes, "I am now nearly convinced that my book will fall flat. The reasons for this belief you will see from my letter to Herbert Read of which I am sending you a copy. It will be a great pity, but it has happened with better books, I believe. For me personally it may mean that I cannot move from my present position, which means spending my life being bullied and humiliated for a salary which is and remains below what we spend, even though we do *not* buy any such luxuries as books or clothes. This is the ninth year that I am doing *all* the teaching in philosophy, and I am the only member of the staff who has not got a salary rise in this time – or rather, there is no member who has not got at least four rises in this period. Still, this would not mean very much if it were not a symptom. The interesting thing is that those of my friends who protested on my behalf against this treatment were told something like this:'We know that he is too good for this place. This we cannot help; and we shall not try to hold him if he wishes to go elsewhere.' It is difficult to explain this strange attitude. It has nothing to do with me, rather with the fact that my mere presence here endangers certain accepted standards; I mean standards of relaxation rather than of work. All Chairs are Easy Chairs here. All this has become much more difficult by the writing of my book, and again, of course, by the delay of the publication."[121]

6. The Book's Publication

On February 29, 1944, Gombrich hastily wrote to Popper, "Last Thursday I got a letter from Herbert Read, who is one of the co-directors of Routledges saying that he read your MS and is '*tremendously impressed*' and asking me for some more information about you which he can use in trying to convince his colleagues."[122] This was not only the beginning of a co-operative effort which led to the publication of *The Open Society*, but also of a publishing relationship between Popper and Routledge which would last more than half a century. Gombrich met with Hayek and Read in the Reform Club and reported the outcome of the conversation to Popper: "Read, who is a man of absolute integrity, offered to publish either one abridged volume or the whole in two volumes with six months interval between the first and the second. We agreed on the latter. He offers the usual conditions of 10 % royalties on the first sales rising later (I don't know yet after how many volumes) to 15 % and an advance of these royalties of £ 50. As an alternative he would have offered as advance all royalties for the copies subscribed before publication but Hayek advised me to accept the round sum. He does not insist on American rights and is ready to leave the matter in abeyance though as an author he advises you to use their firm as an agency in the U.S.A. – he said he had not done so with his last book and rather regrets it. This, however, may be settled later. He will start setting now but estimates that publication rebus sic stantibus will take nine months (for the first volume). He suggests six months interval because by then the first volume will have been reviewed.

He does not need a power of attorney but would like, for his files, a letter from you to the effect that I am entitled to sign on your behalf."[123]

After the publishing contract (with the above-mentioned conditions) was signed, Popper's primary concern was how quickly both volumes could be released. Gombrich wrote to him on April 10, 1944, "I am trying to find some good English student who could read the proofs and make the index. I am afraid this may cost comparatively much money but I think we need a really good person and they are scarce now. I would not dare to let a foreigner or refugee read English proofs. Or would you? It's mainly the punctuation which is so difficult."[124] In a letter to Braunthal dated April 11, 1944, Popper mentioned as one of his publications "...the new book, accepted for publication by Routledge-Kegan Paul, and to be published probably in 1944, and in any case before April 1945."[125] However, before this was to take place, a whole series of other difficulties would have to be surmounted. On July 21, 1944, Popper wrote a letter to Mr. Read in which he attempted to explain why his book was so "topical and urgent." Popper wrote, among other things, "I feel that nothing is so important at the present time as an attempt to get over the fateful dissension within the camp of the friends of the 'open society', i.e., the camp of humanitarianism; or, if I may say so, within the camp of 'the left', if this term is used to include liberals who appreciate the need for social reform. The ultimate humanitarian aims of this 'left', and the sincerity of the vast majority of its members, seems to me beyond doubt; and yet, within this 'left', there is perhaps more internal quarrel, more suspicion, and more reluctance to cooperate, than between the 'left' and the 'right'. My book was written in an attempt to emphasize the unity of the humanitarian camp and to criticize its mistakes in form of a self-criticism." He went on to express his fears that there might be delays, especially in the release of the first volume – and what could be "a more urgent and more important task for a political book, at the present moment" than "...clearing the air within the camp of humanitarianism"?[126]

As early as August 25, 1944, Gombrich was able to telegraph Popper: "Routledges start printing second volume within next month", which put Popper in an embarrassing situation, for he had not only completely rewritten the 17th chapter, but had, in the meantime, made extensive additional corrections on volume two. How could the publishing deadline be met under these circumstances? Popper writes, "With a truly heroic effort I have tried to finish the extremely important corrections to vol. II. I know I have asked you already too much; but now I implore you (I sincerely hope it is the last time) to do everything in your power to get these corrections into the book ... My whole heart is in them."[127] He was willing to pay 30 pounds or more in order to get these corrections incorporated into the book without any delays in the publication. Eight days later he added, "I do want at least a number of the corrections most urgently. I do not want to delay publication!"[128] How this dilemma should be solved, however, he did not say. On October 11, 1944, Gombrich wrote to Popper: "We now have the first 96 pages or so of proofs (and a packet arrives almost every day). They are page proofs and as far as a cursory examination shows the printing is very neat and accurate."

At the beginning of 1945, when the first volume had still not been released, Popper insisted on the fulfillment of the terms of the contract and tried to convince his friend that legal action should now be taken. Popper had found out from a bookseller in Christchurch, who had apparently received his information from Routledge, that *The Open Society* would not be released before the end of 1945. Popper wrote, "Concerning the publication date, I am very much disturbed indeed, although I cannot believe that Routledges should be capable of a procedure bordering on dishonesty. He must know that we (you and I) expect that the book will be published, at the very latest by April, according to contract."[129] Once again, Gombrich proved to be a sober realist when he responded, "The trouble is – I hope you won't consider me cynical or callous – that we are in fact in their hands, since we have no sanctions to apply. Whether they would choose to refer to the corrections or to the labour shortage or to the continuous bombing or to unforeseen difficulties in paper allocation – we can't take the book away from them without risking infinitely more delay. I needn't remind you that 'Power corrupts', even in these matters, and since the difficulties under which they work are, no doubt, very genuine I think we should appeal to their ambition rather than to any legal text."[130] After Gombrich had contacted Routledge concerning the delays in publication, Mr. Ragg replied, "We never fix publication dates now until we have actually had supplies of a book delivered by the binders. There's so much work still to be done in the production of the Open Soc. and conditions in the printing and binding works are so chaotic that I have not the slightest expectation of getting finished copies of the book here until the late Summer or early Autumn of this year. The most probable publication time would therefore be autumn 1945 which shows that the Christchurch bookseller was quite right in giving the end of 1945 as the date of publication. His information probably came from our agent there."[131]

These explanations could not assuage Popper's impatient demand that *The Open Society* be published before the end of the war. In a letter to Gombrich dated February 15, 1945, Popper started by quoting excerpts from the publishing contract. "'The publishers shall, *unless prevented by war* [Popper's emphasis, H.K.], strikes, lock-outs or other circumstances beyond the Publishers' control, within twelve months of the delivery of the complete manuscript, unless otherwise mutually agreed, at their own risk and expense produce and publish the work.'" He then continued, "Since the war is here specifically mentioned we are, of course, legally entirely in their hands. There is no doubt: a legal redress is impossible, we have to try to appeal to their decency, as you suggest. But what actually happened should certainly bind them to publish the *entire work within one year* (as provided in the contract); in fact, *they should have published* (as I shall show you) *the entire work by December or January* ... I am terribly sorry about my complaints but I think if you read all that I have been told about the publication, you will agree that they did not treat us well."[132] Gombrich did not lose his friendly serenity, answering, "I do think you judge a little harshly. Things are difficult and times aren't normal in any way – I know you know that but I am not sure whether you can quite visualise it."[133] On March 9th, he responded to Popper's February 15th letter, writing, "You are, of course, right in many points, perhaps in all. The only thing where I do not quite agree with you is that the delay came as a surprise and that it would have been Ragg's duty to warn us about it. Perhaps it was my fault that I did not warn you but I thought I had kept you pretty well en courant as to the arrival of proofs and their despatch and since the first proofs of vol. I only arrived in October I was not very surprised that a delay was 'in the offing'. However, it is quite possible that there was some muddle but more likely than not, if there was one, I share in the responsibility for it ..."[134]

On May 4, 1945, four days before the complete surrender of the German forces, Popper wrote to Gombrich, "When this letter reaches you, V-E-day will be over. With this, any legal or moral excuse for Routledge to delay the publication any longer disappears. Would you write him that I am pressing you to ask for a definite promise to publish the book not later than a certain (early) date? I think that two months should be ample, since the book is set up. Paper shortage is no excuse: he gets his quota, and it was his duty to reserve paper for the book before the contract expired. Please excuse that I am writing like this: I am so exasperated and unhappy about the fate of the book, and I am sure that Routledges have treated me badly." When Gombrich received this letter, the war in Europe was not only over, but the decision to offer Popper the post at the LSE had already been made. On May 30, 1945, Gombrich thus responded, "It may well be that your approach in person will put the fear of God into them [Routledges, H.K.] if your suspicion is right that they need prodding. Of course you must agree that your reading of the case (including the coincidence of my plea and the arrival of the proofs) is 'an interpretation' and that the facts on which it is based are scanty. As you know the most notorious bottle neck in publication is not shortage of paper but of labour (particularly for binding) and you are going to see that soon for yourself. Still, there can be no harm in setting upon them from all quarters."

About one month later, on July 2, 1945, Popper contacted Herbert Read once again with a "latest epistle", as he referred to it in a letter to Ernst Gombrich, concerning the release of his book in the U.S.A. and England. Among other things, he wrote, "I was, of course, terribly disappointed about the part of your letter that refers to the publication in England; so much so that I can hardly say anything about it. You say that my book will not loose by being postponed until the elections are over. If I could interpret this as a promise that my book will be published *immediately after the elections*, then it would not be too bad. But I am afraid you did not intend to promise me anything in your letter ... I know from Dr. Gombrich that you were very interested in my book, and that your decision to publish it quickly in spite of its length was not an easy one at the time. Believe me that I shall never forget this; your kindness towards my book means for me rather more than kindness towards myself. But the pressure of new problems and the adventure of new discoveries cannot fail to distract your immediate attention from my book; and I feel that I cannot avoid reminding you that once your decision was taken to publish the book in spite of its length, the great amount of paper needed must not be allowed to count against it, difficult as matters may be ...

Please accept my apologies for this long and sad tirade; and believe me that it was much more difficult and painful for me to write this letter than it can possibly be for you to read it."[135]

In the meantime, on June 27th, T. Murray Ragg had written the following to Gombrich, among other things: "'I was glad to hear of Dr. Popper's appointment as Reader ... and all being well publication of his book should coincide approximately to the date of his taking up his work in London Univ. Indeed, if the book is not out in October it should be within a very short time afterwards', upon which Gombrich replied on June 28th, "I quite agree with you that no second proofs should be submitted if, as you say, it adds so immensely to the already great delays of production. I share with you your confidence in your printers whose accuracy I had occasion to admire. Had it been possible I would have exchanged a small number of words against words of slightly better choice but they concern small matters which would not warrant a day's delay in publication'." On July 2nd, Ragg responded to Gombrich, "'I am sorry that you are disappointed about the publication date ... and I regret to have to say that the reason is that while our paper ration has been slightly increased, conditions in printing and binding works are far worse than they have been at any time during the last four years. Only this morning I have received reports from two of our printers to the effect that they cannot do any further printing for us until March of 1946, because of the immense amount of priority work they have got to put through for the Army Education Scheme. That is the difficulty we are up against. Dr. Popper's book, fortunately, will not be affected by either of these reports, which I only mentioned as typical of conditions today'."[136]

Popper was now determined to proceed differently. He sent a telegram not to Read, but to Routledge, which read: "Wish to protest emphatically against any further delay in publication", and received, much to his amazement, an immediate telegram in reply, which read: "Book now binding. Delay entirely due to printers and binders short staffs. Have used all possible means to expedite. Routledge."[137] Of course, Popper understood this was more of an excuse than a guarantee, but in a letter to Gombrich be wrote, "the apologetic tone of the reply cable is entirely new and shows that as long as one is meek they are rather curt, but when one begins to be curt, they become effusive". Finally, on November 22, 1945, Hayek sent Popper a letter in which he wrote, "As you probably know, your book has appeared last week and – by war-time standards – is exceptionally well produced. I have so far seen no reviews yet."[138] Popper's concerns were not dismissed with this news, for he wrote to Gombrich, "Since the book is now out there will be, I suppose, a few awful reviews available on arrival. But I am determined not to get depressed even about the most appalling reviews."[139] And one other thing had been worrying Popper for quite some time, namely similar ideas found in Hayek's book *The Road to Serfdom*[140], released earlier in 1944, which could lead to his being accused of plagiarism. It was for this reason that he wrote to Gombrich on September 4, 1944, "I wish you to put, after the very end of the *Notes to the second volume,* the following *final remark* in italics (separate paragraph). ++The final manuscript of volume I was completed by October 1942, and that of volume II by February 1943. However, some additions were made during printing.++"[141] These exact remarks can be found on page 346, following all the notes, in the 1945 first edition of *The Open Society*. Upon their release, both volumes together cost £ 2.2s or 42s.

7. The Appointment at the London School of Economics (LSE)

There is no doubt that Popper's impending book *The Open Society and Its Enemies* had a positive, albeit perhaps only indirect, influence on his being offered the position at the LSE made vacant by Prof. Abraham Wolf's 1941 retirement, even though his initial position there was to be a *Readership in Logic and Scientific Method*. On July 12, 1945, Hayek had already written confidentially to Gombrich from Cambridge (where the London School of Economics had been relocated during the war), "I am personally anxious to get Dr. Popper to this School, but so far this is merely a personal wish of mine and unless I can convince some of my colleagues that he combines his recognised competence in Logic and Scientific Method with an active interest in the problems of the social science I have little chance. With the MS in my hand I might do a little more – though I should, of course, be most careful how I use it." [142] And on November 5, 1943, Hayek had officially asked Popper if he would be interested in the position.[143] On January 5, 1945, shortly before the post was to be publicly advertised, Hayek wrote to Gombrich, "If you have a spare set of the proofs of the book, the best thing would probably be to let me have it so that I can take it to the meeting."[144] I would like to go into a little more detail concerning the connection between the publication of Popper's book and his being appointed by the LSE.

On December 9, 1943, Popper wrote to Gombrich, "Dear Ernst, Although this airgraph contains what is undoubtedly very good news for me, and therefore, I know, for you too, it places, I am afraid, another burden on your surely already aching shoulders! My only excuse is that I simply cannot help this. You will at once see why. A few days ago I got a truly overpowering airgraph from Hayek, whose indefatigable kindness to me promises no less than to change the whole course of my life."[145] Indeed, the realization of this plan demanded Ernst Gombrich's complete commitment, since it would be necessary for him to carry out all the formalities directly from England if Popper's applications were to be submitted on time. Popper apparently forsaw this when he wrote, "I *must* trouble you again, much as I should like to spare you. I hope to God that this matter will cause you only little trouble, at least as compared with the book." Little by little, Popper sent Gombrich all application materials, references, his curriculum vitae, etc., which might be necessary, because "the matter may possibly be urgent". However, no decision was made in this matter until after the war had ended. On January 29, 1944, Hayek had already written to Popper, "I fear it will all be very slow and my afterthought of asking you how rapidly you could be available, which may have been misleading, was meant to forestall the danger that, when the matter becomes suddenly urgent, as it well may, your distance may form a serious obstacle. I am very glad that this is not likely to be the case."[146]

Popper immediately put together a letter of application for Ernst Gombrich which read: "Dear Sir, On behalf of Dr. K. R. Popper, of Christchurch, N.Z., I have the honour to submit an application for the post of Reader in Logic and Scientific Method. I enclose a statement by Dr. Popper of his qualifications (Studies, Teaching Experience, and Researches); two recent testimonials from Prof. J. Hight, Pro-Chancellor of the Univ. of N.Z., and from Dr. H.S. Allan, Dean of the Faculty of Science, Canterbury Univ. College; together with certified copies of older testimonials from Bertrand Russell; Niels Bohr; L. Susan Stebbing; R. Carnap; J. E. Findlay; A. Tarski; H. Gomperz; furthermore, a medical certificate of health; and a photograph of Dr. Popper." Of even greater interest, however, is Popper's December 13, 1943 letter to Gombrich, in which we read, "What follows now is confidential: I may say, at this place, that we are, of course, terribly excited and shaken up in consequence of Hayek's airgraph concerning the L.S.E. readership. I do not think that I shall get it, owing to the fact that I have so few publications; but if I don't get it, we shall be, of course, disappointed, much as we try to fortify ourselves against such a development. I was so nicely working along with a new paper on probability, and now: 'My peace is gone, my heart is heavy.' Don't think that I am ungrateful. Nobody can feel more strongly than I feel, about Hayek. He must have worked for me like anything. And the moral effect of this on me is, of course, tremendous. I feel no longer cast away, as I did only a few days ago. But what I am longing for is something different – the publication of the book, which I believe is important, much more than an excellent post (even if I get it), although I should very much like to get this post."[147]

In order to increase Popper's chances of getting the Readership at the London School of Economics, Hayek had to win over influential people who would play a crucial role in the decision-making process.[148] It was for this reason that he gave a copy of Popper's manuscript to Lionel Robbins to read. Gombrich wrote in regards to this, "Hayek ... tells me about his efforts to have you seriously considered for the post at the School, that he got your reply but that the post is a University matter where they can only recommend. 'But I regard the prospects on the whole as good, though it may take quite a long while till anything comes of it'. He very kindly promises me to draw my attention to the advertisement, when it comes, which will 'probably not be before autumn at the earliest'."[149] Gombrich met with Hayek in the Reform Club in London, "amidst guilded columns and white haired gentlemen with pink but angular faces", where Hayek told him that he was "rather optimistic about your post at the L.S.E. though he did not want to raise any false hopes etc. but *if* the post is created at all – and that does not depend on the School – he seems to regard your chances as pretty great."[150] Later, Gombrich wrote to Popper, "The most optimistic interpretation would be that the post was to some extent set up with an eye to appointing you – Hayek certainly persued the matter from the beginning with that possibility in view. The least optimistic interpretation would be that Hayek backs you so strongly with some ulterior motives – e.g. to prevent a candidate of Mannheim's to get in whose influence he would consider detrimental."[151] In addition, Popper had received an offer to take on a philosophy professorship, a "Presbyterian Church chair", at the University of Otago (N.Z.), which came with a salary of about £ 1.000, succeeding John N. Findlay, who was leaving to take up a professorship in South Africa.[152]

On December 30, 1944, John N. Findlay telegraphed Popper: "Philosophy professorship Western Australia Salary starts £ 800 apply before January 15th."[153] Popper had also applied for a low-paying teaching position in Sydney because, as he ironically told Gombrich, "the opportunity of seeing a Koala bear is worth putting up with anything".[154] How could Popper make a decision? It was not until this same January 15, 1945 that Gombrich wrote to inform Popper that, "After a rather protracted period of pregnancy (22 months?)"[155], the London School of Economics had advertised the University Readership in Logic and Scientific Method, with a salary of no less than £ 600. He gave all the details of the advertisement, which he had received from Hayek – in particular that the application deadline was February 26th, and that the interview of the potential candidates, which would obviously be impossible for Popper to attend, would take place on March 21st. Hayek had written to Gombrich, "... the final decision will presumably be made on that latter day, and though officially it will have to go first to the Senate, I shall try to get permission to inform Dr. Popper at once of the result."[156] The appointment was to take effect on October 1, 1945, the Senate reserving the right to decide whether it would be for a limited period or last until retirement. Gombrich felt the salary to be sufficient – it was comparable to his own – "though I won't pretend that the Agha Khan [does not have] a greater margin", even though Popper would have to pay more income tax than Gombrich, who had one child. Gombrich did not lose his sense of humor, even when the appointment situation at the London School became precarious. On February 8, 1945, he wrote, "Since you got me used to reading the adverts in the Times I have made the discovery that no other profession is in such demand as philosophers. (Or are they in such short supply?). When you come to England you should definitely train Richard [Gombrich's son, H.K.] in that occupation, it seems to be the most lucrative I know of."[157]

The complications, however, did not come to an end. When the meeting of the LSE board to decide on who would receive the post was delayed for several days, Hayek was unable to postpone his lecture trip to the U.S.A.[158] Gombrich telegraphed Popper on March 23, 1945: "Contacting registrar Hayeks American journey endangering quick notification" and wrote in a letter one day earlier, "Well these developments and constant complications gradually remind me of the stage rather than of reality, though I am sure that you as the passive 'hero' of that play won't exactly enjoy its knots and intricacies."[159] Popper answered on March 28th, "This cable, by the way, was a very heavy blow. Hayek's absence must reduce my L.S.E. prospects very much indeed."[160] In response to Gombrich's inquiries, the responsible administrator at the LSE was merely able to say that he would perhaps know by the end of April when a decision could be expected, upon which Gombrich wrote to Popper, "This U.S. journey of Hayek's 'hat uns noch gefehlt'[was just what we needed]."[161]

Popper wrote to Hayek on April 11, 1945, "I was very disappointed when I heard about the mishap preventing you to be in England when the decision about the readership was made ... If the decision should be favourable, I shall owe this entirely to you".[162] At the beginning of May, Popper commented to Gombrich, "So many thanks for your cable saying that the decision is expected by the end of April: I got it 'by the end of April' i.e. on the last, and until now I have not heard any more about it. I begin to think that they must have appointed somebody else; they never bother to inform the unsuccessful candidates. It is now *eighteen* months since we are more or less in suspense about it."[163]

Karl Popper himself reported how he received a telegram on May 21, 1945, with the news that he had been chosen for the position at the LSE.[164] On May 17, 1945, Gombrich wrote Popper a happy, ironic letter in which he began, "Today I got a letter from Hayek who is just back from the USA and who says that he has heard to his great satisfaction that you have been appointed, mentions your letter to him of April 11 and wonders whether any concrete steps have already been taken etc. I need hardly tell you how glad I was – having waited for more than a month for every mail (luckily there is only one a day) whether the Registrar would finally condescend to let me know."[165] The official telegram arrived on May 28th: "University London offers you Readership Logic salary sevenhundred and fifty pounds".[166] Popper took up his new post at the LSE at the beginning of 1946, holding it for three years before being appointed Professor of Logic and Scientific Method in 1949.

Before immigrating to England, one major difficulty proved to be Popper's naturalization as an English citizen. On December 22, 1943, Popper had already written to Gombrich, "It lately occurred to me that Hayek might assume that I have been naturalized; but I am not ... I have asked *twice* to be naturalized: First in 1938 (immediately before the invasion of Austria) but was told, in a letter from the Office of the Minister of Internal Affairs, dated March 7, 1938 (I. A. 115/57) that 5 years residential qualifications are statutory. In 1941, I applied again (having fulfilled these qualifications); and I received a reply, dated Nov. 3rd 1941 (same number), saying: 'I have to acknowledge receipt of your letter of the 28th ultimo relative to your desire to become naturalized as a British subject. In reply I have to inform you that the Government has discontinued the granting of naturalization during the war period and it is regretted that no such applications are being considered at the present time.' – I may say that, at the time, I was already officially classified as a friendly alien, and as 'stateless' (without nationality), and that the Alien Authority had strongly recommended me for earliest naturalization, as soon as that is possible."[167] And on July 2, 1945, Popper informed Hayek of his difficulties in leaving New Zealand, writing, among other things, that "[a] special difficulty will be the passports. The passport office in Christchurch told me that the case of an alien going to England has not occurred to them before, and that they do not know what to do about it."[168]

In addition, Hennie and Karl Popper needed emigration permits. Popper told Gombrich in a letter dated July 24, 1945, "Within 53 days of my applying for a permit to leave NZ, I have made *no* progress whatever: I was not able to elicit any reply from the authorities apart from the cyclostyled acknowledgement of the receipt of my application." Therefore, he traveled to Wellington in person, where he learnt that London University, the administrative authority of the LSE, had not yet submitted an application for his entrance permit to England. "Under these circumstances we shall *certainly* not be able to leave before October."[169] In Wellington Popper was told that the New Zealand High Commissioner in London had yet to be informed of this matter by London University, and that an *English Entrance Permit* was, therefore, lacking. Popper informed Hayek accordingly with a telegram on the 25th of July and a letter on the 26th, who, in turn, responded by telegram on July 29th: "Cable sent from HC Office and necessary steps arranged here."[170] One month later, nothing had changed substantially. Popper writes, "Our departure problems are appalling and ... we probably won't be in England before the beginning of December: we have still no permits to enter Great Britain and I begin to fear that we won't get any. I am, of course, in continuous contact about this with Hayek who says that London University administration has completely broken down. Apparently they have not applied for our permits so far! This blocks things here. Result: an awful muddle."[171]

However, all the difficulties were gradually resolved. On September 7, 1945, London University telegraphed: "Home Office authorises visa facilities yourself and wife New Zealand Government informed."[172] At the same time, however, a further complication arose, in that the entrance visa was to be limited to 12 months. Popper wrote to Hayek, "The news that we are to get only visitor's permits for twelve months is a very severe blow ... this would mean, in effect, that if I now go to England, I may not know where to go after the war is over. For I have certainly no intention of returning to Austria, and it is one of my main aims in this life to attain the status of a British subject."[173] After the Poppers had left Christchurch on October 16th, Popper finally sent a hand-written letter to Gombrich from Auckland on November 14th, 1945, which read, "*One* very good thing has happened – the Government decided to re-introduce the practise of naturalization and we were, indeed, the first to be naturalized. Thus we shall arrive (if we ever arrive) as British Subjects. We have British Passports – - but no tickets!"[174] Two days later, Popper was able to inform Gombrich that they would be departing for England aboard the M.V. 'New Zealand Star' in a four-bed cabin between November 28th and December 5th. "We are not terribly pleased to pay £ 320 for the pleasure of spending 5 or 6 very rough weeks in the company of strangers. I am particularly concerned about the fact that I cannot endure the smell of cigarettes at sea without getting sick – still, I shall have to get used to it."[175]

8. The Book's Success

On December 2, 1945,[176] the Poppers' ship left New Zealand and arrived in Southampton at the beginning of January 1946, where the Gombrichs awaited them with a copy of *The Open Society*, which Popper "eagerly scrutinised on the train and bus to [Gombrichs', H.K.] little semi-detached house in Brent".[177] Although World War II had been over for six months, post war bottlenecks were the rule in England, as far as living conditions were concerned. On March 4, 1945, Ernst Gombrich wrote, "Regarding furniture etc. Take with you *as much as you possibly can* of any kind of household goods, furniture etc., and, I think, *don't* sell the rest but store it with friends for the time when one can ship it. You probably can't imagine the scarcity of civilian commodities from pots and pans to toilet paper or razor blades. Furniture is practically unobtainable. To buy new 'utility' furniture requires a permit and second hand furniture is not only very scarce but goes for truly fantastic prices. A second-hand bed £ 50 and things of that kind ... As for curtains, bedspreads etc. You have either to buy rationed material (which you can't because it would soon swallow up all your coupons) or the exceptional type of material which isn't rationed and is unsuitable and terribly expensive ... So if you come here bring all you can. Hairpins are exceedingly scarce, combs *absolutely* unobtainable, blankets, towels, household linen are veritable treasures. Well, I think you are in the picture now."[178]

All these difficulties were of secondary significance, however, for Karl Popper was now not only in England, the nation of his choice, but his book was also receiving ever-increasing notice and attention. At this point I would like to quote just a few excerpts from reviews during the first year after the book's release in order to demonstrate that the publication of

The Open Society fulfilled almost all of Popper's expectations, and quickly made him well-known as a political philosopher. On December 9, 1945, The *Sunday Times* published a short discussion of the book – "of so large a work must necessarily be a bad review" – written by Sir Ernest Barker, where we also read, "There is an abundance of riches in the book – classical scholarship, scientific acumen, logical subtlety, philosophical sweep."[179] And on January 12, 1946, H. St. Lawrence wrote in *Time and Tide*, "It seems a pity to have to say 'non tali auxilio' to so earnest a fighter in the cause of humanism and democracy. Nor can a brief notice hope to do justice to his wide-ranging arguments, so simply and forcefully presented in these volumes, in which there is much to invite agreement." A few days later, on January 18th, George Woodcock wrote in the *Tribune*, "Here is an important book which I hope will be read even by those who will hardly agree with the author's main conclusions." Woodcock described Popper's book as "stimulating and iconoclastic". In contrast, Lord Linsay wrote on January 25th in *The Manchester Guardian Weekly* that he believed the two volumes were too extensive and as a result, although the work was interesting, it would be a book which, "comparatively few people [would] read"! He went on to criticize "Dr. Popper's fierce heresy-hunting" in a book that was "well worth reading".

The first longer, seven page review appeared in the May 1946 edition of *Polemic*, written by Hugh Trevor-Roper. He saw Popper's book as "a protest closely reasoned" against the history of political totalitarianism since Plato. Popper's attacks on the three great tyrants of philosophy, Plato, Hegel, and Marx, were carried by a rationale that was founded upon a belief: "His own faith is the faith of the great sophists of the fifth century BC, whose plea that man is the measure of all things is still audible through the narcotic incantations, the transcendental idealism, with which Plato sought to overwhelm it." After Trevor-Roper presented in detail the most important conclusions of both volumes, he ended by writing, "It is a magnificent and a timely achievement; and I consider his book as by far the most important work of contemporary sociology. He has utterly demolished the philosophical basis of historicism, which still has so many practical and theoretical devotees; he has restored politics and institutions to fundamental human importance, since it is they which give form and human significance to what is otherwise an objective natural phenomenon; and, by a necessary derivation, he has restored significance to human choice and the human will." In October 1946, Hugh N. Parton published a review of several pages in the *Staff Newsletter* of the University of New Zealand, which began with the statement, "This book is a part, and worthy part, of New Zealand's war effort." Parton, who, in 1945, had published a pamphlet entitled *Research and the University*[180] in Christchurch along with Popper and Robin S. Allan, was convinced that few readers "[would] lay his work aside unenlightened about the influence of ideas on human history, and, one may hope, unconvinced of the necessity of applying the critical methods of science to the problems of social reform". And as a friend and physical chemist, Parton wrote of Popper, "The author would rather be called a scientist than a philosopher. He would be proud to claim the title of democrat. His book is a testament of democracy ... Dr. Popper's influence will remain with us. It may even prove decisive in the future of the social sciences, if his example is followed." Julius Kraft wrote in *The Saturday Review of Literature* (USA), appearing on November 5, 1946, "This formidable task [of an intellectual purification, H.K.] is approached with a sincerity and originality of judgement seldom to be found in contemporary writing on political philosophy."

In October 1943, Hayek had written to Popper concerning the book, "I am most anxious for it to come out soon and be a real success",[181] two wishes, of which at least the latter would prove to come true. While Popper had written to Rudolf Carnap from Vienna on October 23, 1932, "You once made the comment in Burgstein, which is apparently quite correct, that I am overly sensitive due to a lack of success",[182] with the success of his book, Popper's academic career now entered a new stage. And it was again Carnap, who had sent many books and articles to Popper in Christchurch, who wrote to Popper from Chicago on February 9, 1946, after receiving a copy of *The Open Society*, "I am certain that your book will find very much interest among readers in both philosophy and political science in this country...

I was so enthusiastic about your book that I immediately called the attention of our whole department to it, and also that of a group of young teachers of social science in the college who are now considering it for use in the big Social Science Survey Course. I suppose that your book will stir up lively controversies. It may be that the majority of philosophers will be strongly opposed to it, chiefly because of the debunking of Plato. But that does not matter. It is at present more important for your book to find attention than to find agreement. The fact that it will often be discussed, even if sharply criticized, will be sufficient for calling the attention of young people to it, and this is, of course, what actually matters." Almost a half century later, there is little that one can add to Carnap's assessment.

© Hubert Kiesewetter

Notes

* Without the generous assistance of Sir Ernst Gombrich, Dr. Manfred Lube, and Melitta Mew in the procurement and restoration of Popper's correspondence, I would have been unable to write this article. The majority of the letters used were made available to me in the form of copies from the Karl Popper Collection of the University Library of Klagenfurt. I owe many thanks to David Miller, Alan Musgrave, Peter Munz, John Watkins, and Frank Zschaler for important tips. Likewise, I would like to express my deep gratitude to the legal heirs of Karl Popper's estate and copyright holders, Melitta and Raymond Mew, as well as to Sir Ernst Gombrich for giving me their kind permission to quote from Popper's correspondence. Since some scholars have used the same archival material here quoted, I would like to mention that I finished this article already in 1998, and have sent it for publication to quite a number of people.

1 Cf. Terentianus Maurus, *De litteris syllabis et metris liber*. Recensuit Carolus Lachmannus, Berolini, 1836, p. 44, line 1286: "pro captu lectoris habent sua fata libelli", which I would like to translate: "From the reader's viewpoint, books have their own fate." A somewhat different translation can be found in Terentianus Maurus, *De syllabis*. Edited, translated, and commentated by Jan-Wilhelm Beck, Göttingen, 1993, p. 123. I consider the question as to whether the phrase truly reflects Terentianus' original intention, which Beck insists upon on p. 518-19, to be a fruitless argument of interpretation. It is definitely possible to interpret lines 1291-1293 as I have done.

2 Cf. Karl R. Popper, *Unended Quest: An Intellectual Autobiography*, Glasgow: Collins, 1976, pp. 113-120. Popper treats the three worlds theory, for example, in his essay "On the Theory of the Objective Mind, in: *Objective Knowledge: An Evolutionary Approach*, Oxford: Clarendon Press, 1972, pp. 153-190.

3 Ernst Gombrich, *The Open Society and Its Enemies:* Remembering Its Publication Fifty Years Ago, London, 1995. I have likewise made use of several excerpts from letters reproduced there with the number of the archive files of the Hoover Institution.

4 Popper Archives, Hoover Institution, Stanford University (28,7). Italics found in the original. On August 24, 1943, Alfred Braunthal wrote to Karl Popper: "When I began to read your manuscript, I planned to confine the reading to those chapters which you had advised me to read and to glance through the rest of the book. But hardly had I begun to read it when I radically scratched this plan. So deeply was I moved by your writing, so excited was I and even thrilled that I devoured the entire book as it were in one gulp.
It is hard to convey to you the deep impression your book has made on me and the gratitude with which I have received it ... But what I owe to your book, is the epistemological insight in the errors and dangers of oracular philosophy and is, furthermore, the revelation of the untenability of historicism and of its fundamental immorality." (Ibid., 28,2).
On December 13, 1943, Popper wrote to Gombrich: "The very fact that a man like Hayek – a true liberal, and leading anti-Socialist – and, on the other hand, half Marxists and Socialists like Braunthal and Lasky, agree with the views

expressed in the book seems to show that I have achieved my main aim: the elimination of the largely metaphysical and unreal theoretical differences that stand between all those who are, fundamentally, equalitarians and liberals. Few things can be more important at the moment than a contribution towards such a consolidation of what might be called 'the left'." (300,2)

5 Popper, *Autobiography,* (see note 2), p. 113.
6 Concerning Popper's other scientific work in Christchurch, cf. Jeremy Shearmur, *The Political Thought of Karl Popper,* London, New York: Routledge, 1996, pp. 22-36, as well as Jeremy Shearmur, "Popper, Hayek, and the Poverty of Historicism Part I: A Largely Bibliographical Essay," in: *Philosophy of the Social Sciences,* Vol.28, No.3, 1998, pp.434-450.
7 Popper, *Autobiography,* (see note 2), p. 119, writes: "The book had been written in trying circumstances; libraries were severely limited, and I had had to adjust myself to whatever books were available.", which could therefore be interpreted to mean that the *trying circumstances* referred to a lack of relevant literature.
8 Popper Archives (282,24). Carnap's and Popper's letter is in the original in German.
I have corrected small typing errors in the English letters without any special notation. When it is clear from the context that the quoted excerpts originate from the same archive file, person, and year that was previously mentioned, I have chosen, in the interest of space, to *no longer* include "Ibid." with the source.
9 Original German quoted by Max Domarus, *Hitler. Reden und Proklamationen 1932-1945.* Kommentiert von einem deutschen Zeitgenossen. Bd. I: Triumph, 2. Halbband 1935-1938, Wiesbaden: Löwith, 1973, p. 823.
10 Popper Archives (300,2). Letter from Hennie Popper to Ernst and Ilse Gombrich on July 29, 1943, p. 3: "No one who has not lived on an island half way to the moon can realize what it means to try to get in contact with the world."
11 Popper Archives (300,2).
12 Popper Archives (282,24).
13 Popper Archives (305,13).
14 Therefore, Ingrid Belke is incorerect when she maintains in "Karl R. Popper im Exil in Neuseeland von 1937 bis 1945," in: Friedrich Stadler (Ed.), *Vertriebene Vernunft II: Emigration und Exil österreichischer Wissenschaft 1930-1940,* Wien, München: Jugend und Volk, 1988, p. 145, that "the major expenses in the family budget disappeared" after the purchase of the house. Cf. also below, p. 4, and note 19.
15 Popper Archives (300,2). Letter written on July 29, 1943, p. 1. Next quote, p. 2.
16 Ernst Gombrich responded on October 13, 1943, "I also want to thank Henny very much for the graphic though somewhat saddening picture of your life – it makes one feel rather ashamed of living in such undeserved (comparative) luxury." (Ibid.) and added later, on December 7, "If it were not for the rather inconvenient hours of my work (mostly from 6. p.m. to 2.30. a.m.) which I find a little exhausting there would be nothing left to be desired except the end of the war. But this very much so."

17 Cf. Hacohen, "Karl Popper in Exile", (see note 109), p. 458. John Watkins, "Karl Raimund Popper 1902-1994," in: *Proceedings of the British Academy*, Vol. 94, 1997, p. 652, reports that Felix Kaufmann worked on behalf of Popper, so that he was granted a possibility to work as an academic guest at Cambridge, "for one year at £ 150".

18 Popper Archives (300,4).Italics found in the original. In the same letter he wrote concerning the travel costs to England, "These will be very high – berths alone about 310 N.Z. £, shifting of furniture, insurance etc. about 70 £; to this we must add that we shall have to pay two years income tax before leaving: t he pay-as-you-go tax system does not exist yet, although it will probably be introduced next year. This means another 100 £. In brief, leaving N.Z. will cost us 500 N.Z. £!" On August 25, 1945, he complained to Gombrich, "I wonder why one has always to worry about money?" (Ibid.)

19 Popper Archives (28,7). Letter from June 29, 1943, p. 3. On May 21, 1943, Popper had already written to Hellin, "We have extremely little money, or more precisely, considerable debts, and live accordingly. One of our rare pleasures is that a friend has given us a wireless and that we sometimes (for example to-day) hear Rudi [Serkin, H.K.] and Busch; but we have very rarely time to listen." (Ibid., p. 1)

20 Popper Archives (28,6). Enclosure B, p. 3. Italics in original.

21 Popper Archives (300,2). On June 17, 1943, Gombrich had already written to Popper, "It is very kind of you to send me some money to cover the expenses but I really would not have wanted you to take all this trouble since I am for the time being a member of the plutocratic caste and the settlements of these accounts could easily have waited till after the war."

22 Popper Archives (300,3). Popper to Gombrich, October 24, 1944. The letter was originally filed under 305,13 by mistake. On September 24, 1944, after the publication of Part I of *The Poverty of Historicism* in "Economica" , Popper had written to Hayek, "I must also thank you for the cheque – the first payment for a literary effort since 1935, and the largest I ever received!" (305,13)

23 Cf. as well, below, p. 28 and note 157.

24 Popper Archives (300,4). Popper to Gombrich, February 10, 1945.

25 Popper Archives (28,7).

26 Popper Archives (300,2).

27 Popper Archives (28,2), p. 4.

28 Ibid. Braunthal had been quite concerned about Popper's health and wrote, relieved, on April 2nd, "Am I right in concluding from your last letter, Karl, that your sickness consisted in tooth trouble? We are, of course, very sorry about [that], but at least I don't feel as disquiet any more as I felt after your previous letter in which you just intimated that something was wrong with your health." Popper responded on June 19, "You very kindly inquire about my health. It is not only tooth-ache which troubles me; the abscesses on my teeth constitute, rather, only one of the many symptoms of a physical (not nervous) break down due to exhaustion (so the doctor says)", and Braunthal answered on July 29th, "Karl don't let it be a wishdream, keep yourself up for your further work, for your wife, for the world which needs you and for your friends."

29 Popper Archives (300,3). On June 27, 1944, he wrote, "I am still extremely weak and feeble. The doctor says that I had the lowest blood pressure he has

ever seen. This explains why I feel as I do. I am now taking five different pills several times a day and I get injections too."
30 Ibid. Gombrich to Popper, June 10, 1944. Popper replied on July 12th, "I wished you were right in your diagnosis that I work too much: unfortunately, I can't work at all, at present, which is a depressing state of affairs and in so far a vicious circle. And I wish I could follow your advice and not give so many lectures. This is, however, impossible." Later, Gombrich repeated his inquiry. "First of all I want to know how you are and whether your method of treating your complaints is wise and becoming to a critical rationalist?" (Ibid. Gombrich to Popper, August 4, 1944).
31 Popper Archives (300,2). Letter dated July 29, 1943, p. 2. Later, Hennie continues, "Karl finished just two days before College started again. On both days which remained from our 'holidays' we went to the sea and ate as many icecreams as we could (I had planned it long ago that we would celebrate the end with eating as many icecreams as we wanted). The first day went off quite well but on the second day we got caught in a thunderstorm which ended our celebration abruptly. And Karl went to start a new year in College and I went back to an entirely wrecked and ruined house and garden."
32 Popper Archives (300,3).
33 Popper Archives (300,4). Popper to Gombrich, April 16, 1945.
34 Ibid.
35 Cf. Friedrich Scheu, *Ein Band der Freundschaft. Schwarzwald-Kreis und Entstehung der Vereinigung Sozialistischer Mittelschüler,* Vienna, Cologne, Graz: Hermann Böhlau, 1985, pp. 83-94.
36 Popper Archives (28,7). Popper to Dorian, April 20, 1943, p. 2. Italics in original.
37 Thus, it was not in February 1943 that Popper first sent the manuscript to "his friends in the USA", as mistakenly asserted in Belke, "Karl R. Popper im Exil," (see note 14), p. 150.
38 Popper Archives (28,6). Italics in original.
39 Popper Archives (28,7).
40 On account of these instructions, a difference of opinion arose between Braunthal and Popper. It merits a brief mention because, in my view, it reflects the great degree of respect with which these friends regarded each other. Braunthal wrote to Popper on November 25, 1943, with an openness "on which confidence between friends can rest", "You expected your friends to act like machines and were greatly surprised and depressed when you discovered that they acted like human beings. You sent your friends many dozens of 'instructions' describing in the minutest details how to handle the manuscript and are now upset that they failed to obey these instructions to the letter." Popper responded on December 14, 1943, "First, let me thank you most heartily for this letter. It has made a real difference to me. The only thing I am sorry about, in view of this letter, is the fact that you are, undoubtedly, hurt; and this makes me very sorry indeed. But when I tell you most earnestly that your letter fully satisfies me as far as you and your actions past and present are concerned; that I do accept without the slightest hesitation your explanations; and that I can only hope that your trust in my person is not smaller

than my trust in you: then, I hope, you will forgive me fully." Popper Archives (28,2).
41 Popper Archives (28,6). Letter to Burstein, no date available.
Popper's friends were to send a cover-letter (written by Popper) along with the manuscript to the publishers, which read as follows:
"Dear Sirs,
I wish to submit to you on behalf of the author, my friend Dr. K. R. Popper (University of New Zealand), a manuscript under the title:
'A CRITIQUE OF POLITICAL PHILOSOPHY.'
The book is topical. It is a new social philosophy, containing a critical discussion, from a modern point of view, of the most important contributions to the philosophy of politics and of history since Plato. It views totalitarianism from a new perspective, showing that the totalitarian revolt against civilization is as old as civilization itself. It tries to defend democracy against the criticism of the anti-democratic and totalitarian philosophers (whom it shows to be inspired by Plato, Aristotle, and Hegel); and in meeting these attacks it tries to develop the principles of a democratic policy of social reconstruction, by way of a careful analysis of the philosophical prejudices which impede a practical approach to the problems of reconstruction. In this connection, Plato's and Marx's political philosophies are analysed with great care, and many important passages are newly translated. But the book is not only critical. It treats, more especially, some fundamental problems of method. There is an urgent need for a democratic philosophy to support reconstruction plans; and the book tries to contribute to it.
The author is a philosopher of repute. You can read about his work in John Laird's book *Recent Philosophy* (Home University Library), pp. 187, 189 ff. Born in Vienna in 1902, he was connected with the 'Vienna Circle' of philosophers [in "Enclosure B", p. 4, he wrote, "and was a member of the Viennese Circle of Philosophers", H.K.], and he has been since 1937 Senior Lecturer in Philosophy at Canterbury University College, University of New Zealand. In 1935/36 he was invited to give some lectures in England (Cambridge, Bedford College, Imperial College of Science). He is the author of a number of scientific papers and of a book, *Logik der Forschung,* which was published by Julius Springer in 1935 and which received much attention from the leading English and American philosophical periodicals. Prof. R. Carnap, University of Chicago, and Prof. G. E. Moore, the editor of 'Mind', at present in the Department of Philosophy, Columbia University, New York, know Dr. Popper personally and will be pleased to vouch for his scientific reputation.
In view of the fact that communication with New Zealand is very difficult at present, Dr. Popper has asked me to act as his representative.
[Then *either* (I think this is preferable):]
I am sending you by the same mail the manuscript of the text of the book and a sample of the Notes, namely the notes to chapters 2 and 10. The length of the book is about 280.000 words, the notes included.
[Or:]
Should you be interested in seeing the manuscript, I shall be pleased to send it to you. I enclose with this letter, for your further information, the Preface,

Table of Contents, and the Introduction, as well as a stamped envelope. The length of the book is about 280.000 words, the notes included.
Yours faithfully
Address."
In addition, the following conditions were to be agreed upon in the negotiating and signing of a publishing contract:
"Concerning the agreement with the publisher, I may mention that what I know about these matters I have got from a book which may interest you: The Authors Handbook, edited by D. Kilham Roberts (I have the edition of 1938).
(a) The publisher must agree to secure the U.S.A. Copyright in my name
(b) the publishers are obliged to publish within a definite time (I think not more than 4 months, but if necessary up to six months)
(c) the agreement is to be a royalty agreement. I do not mind how small the royalties are for the first 500 or 600 copies, but I want them to increase very considerably after that, and especially should more than 2000 copies be sold.
(d) Translation rights are mine
(e) Licenses for England and the Colonies have to be considered.
Furthermore, if possible:
(f) The publishers shall look after the proof-reading, i.e. obtain an experienced proof-reader who corrects the proofs according to the MS, and to the Instructions I enclose with the MS I am sending you.
If that cannot be done, you may perhaps find somebody to read the proofs carefully ...
My *main interest* is that the book is published *soon* by a *good* publisher. (Ibid., Italics in original). Slightly different conditions can be found in ibid., "Enclosure B", p. 3 f.

42 Popper Archives (28,7). Popper to Hellin, May 15, 1943. Italics and bold print in original. On May 21, 1943, he adds, "You may think me fussy in asking you to keep the MS confidential. But it is one of the most important wishes I have in this matter, and I have a right to ask that it is complied with. The book attacks very vigorously a number of fashionable philosophies, e.g. your friend Mannheim, and the Hegelians, Aristotelians, Wittgensteinians, Bergsonians, Husserlians, and many more. It will *not* be well received by most academic people. And I do not like to have answers to my attacks before the attacks are launched. But there are many other reasons why I wish it to be kept as confidential, and why non-academic people, and even personal friends, are no exception." Italics in original.

43 Popper Archives (28,2). In the telegram, Popper had underlined "untimely" and placed a large exclamation mark above it. On July 22, 1943, he wrote to Gombrich concerning the chances of his book being published in the USA, "In brief, the situation is not only hopeless, but worse. Since January 7th, when the MS was rejected by Macmillan, to whom I sent it myself, it was lying idle, and no one there has ever sent it to any publisher, up to this moment; at least this I found out for certain, after spending a fortune on cables." Popper Archives (300,2).

44 Popper Archives (28,2), Enclosure B, p. 1. He wrote to Frederick Dorian on April 20, 1943, "I feel sure that the reason for the two rejections is the present situation in which people are scared to attack Marx." (28,7)
45 Popper Archives (28,4). Popper to Condliffe, May 19, 1943. Popper added, "Please excuse my sending the MS with this letter, instead of waiting until invited by you to do so; the latter procedure would take too much time; and you can easily get rid of the MS by sending it on to Dr. Braunthal." The letter in response, written by the secretary of Dr. Condliffe, Patricia O'Quin, can also be found here.
46 Cf. John B. Condliffe, *The Reconstruction of World Trade. A Survey of International Economic Relations,* New York: W. W. Norton, 1940.
47 Popper Archives (28,7). Letter dated May 15, 1943.
48 Popper most likely took the names and addresses of the American publishers from *The Authors Playwrights & Composers Handbook for 1938.* Compiled and Edited by D. Kilham Roberts, London: John Lane the Bodley Head, 1938, pp. 216-236.
49 He added "You may be astonished to find the Oxford University Press near the end of my list, and none of the other University Presses mentioned; and indeed, I would prefer an ordinary good publisher to the University Presses, since their imprint might tend to discourage many readers of the type I wish to reach." Popper Archives (28,6). Enclosure B, p. 2.
50 Ibid., p. 2.
51 Popper Archives (28,7). Dorian to Popper, June 26, 1943.
52 Cf. Popper, *Autobiography,* (see note 2), p. 113 and Karl R. Popper, *The Poverty of Historicism,* London: Routledge, 1957, p. IV.
53 Popper Archives (28,2). Popper to Braunthal, May 21, 1943, p. 1. He had apparently also considered Hellin, who probably had less interest in reading the book. "This point is so important because in a time like the present, personal friendship to the author must be less important than the realization that the book is an important contribution to the problems of our time." (Ibid., p. 1 f.)
54 Ernst Gombrich wrote on July 11, 1943, "I also want to tell you that Prof. Saxl, with whom I spent my leave, is a friend of Dr. Julius Braunthal and I wrote to him immediately asking for Alfred Braunthal's address, which I'll let you have as soon as I get it." Popper Archives (300,2). On July 21, he telegraphed Braunthal's address to Popper.
55 Popper Archives (28,7). Popper to Hellin, May 21, 1943, p. 2. Italics in original.
56 Popper Archives (28,2). Popper to Braunthal, May 21, 1943, p. 1.
57 Popper Archives (28,2). Braunthal to Popper, August 24, 1943. Cf. also note 4.
58 Ibid. Braunthal to Popper, July 25, 1943.
59 Braunthal wrote Popper a day later, "After having read your manuscript, I am very optimistic about these chances [of its publication, H.K.], much more than I was after my conversation with Condliffe." (Ibid., August 24, 1943)
60 Cf. Popper Archives (28,2). Braunthal to Popper, November 11, 1943. There we read on p. 2, "You have got two offers, one from a decent and respected commercial publisher, the other from one of the leading University Presses. But publishers agree in the salient point that publication could be considered

only with substantial cuts. I am convinced that no commercial publisher could be found in this country who would think differently." The book had to be cut to 250-300 pages, something which Popper refused to accept.
61 Popper Archives (28,3).
62 Ibid., Braunthal to Popper, May 19, 1944. And later on in this letter we read, "Karl, I am very, very happy – although my American patriotism has received a blow when it turned out that British publishers, inspite of the severe paper crisis over there, are much more easily ready to publish a voluminous manuscript, once its value has been ascertained, than American publishers are, whose market is three times as large as that of English publishers."
63 Popper Archives (28,2). Popper to Braunthal, August 23, 1943. The next quote is from the same source.
64 Cf. my March 27, 1998 interview with Sir Ernst and Lady Gombrich concerning their friendship with Sir Karl Popper. It was in the spring of 1936 in London that Karl Popper really got to know Ernst Gombrich; he was, therefore, not an "old Viennese friend", as I. C. Jarvie and Jeremy Sheamur claim in the "Introduction to the Special Issue: The 50th Anniversary of Popper's The Open Society and Its Enemies," in: *Philosophy of the Social Sciences*, Vol. 26, No. 4, 1996, p. 445.
65 Popper Archives (300,1). Apparently Sir Ernst Gombrich could no longer remember this when he wrote in 1995 that Popper "got my address almost fortuitously, thanks to a common acquaintance". Cf. Gombrich, *The Open Society and Its Enemies,* (see note 3), p. 3.
66 Popper Archives (300,2). My italics. Popper already knew what he was asking of Gombrich in early 1944, when he wrote, "It appears that the position of being my 'friend in England' [Hayek had referred to Gombrich as such, H.K.] is equivalent, although perhaps not to a full-time job, but certainly to a very full part-time job. I wonder how you can carry on with it aside of your other and more immediate duties." (300,3). Popper to Gombrich, January 11, 1944.
67 Cf. Ernst H. Gombrich, *Myth and Reality in German War-Time Broadcasts*, London: Athlone Press, 1970 (The Creighton Lecture in History 1969).
68 Popper Archives (300,2). And on June 22, 1943, he added, "Excuse me please if I continue to bombard you with Airmail letters. But I am a bit nervous whether you got my Airgraph of May 4th in which I explained that, since I do not wish that K. Mannheim be approached in connection with the book, you should either not approach Kegan Paul-Routledge at all, or only at a later date, after others have turned it down ... In any case, I don't want K. Mannheim, and Routledge will therefore be not very adequate as a publisher"! (Ibid.) On July 18, 1943, Hayek had already written to Gombrich, "The Mannheim problem would by itself be no obstacle against approaching Routledge – I am probably treating Mannheim much more rudely in my own book [*The Road to Serfdom*, London, 1944, H.K.] than Dr. Popper is likely to do." (400,6). After the book had been accepted by Routledge, this issue was again addressed by publishing director Herbert Read. Gombrich wrote conerning this, "Read broached the Mannheim question once more – he said M. was quite tolerant and it might be in your interest to have it in that series since many libraries would subscribe it automatically ... but personally he or they were (*confidentially*) quite pleased to do an independent book because he

was gradually taking over the whole firm." (300,3). Gombrich to Popper, March 21, 1944. Italics in original.
69 Popper Archives (300,2). Gombrich to Popper, May 11, 1943.
70 Popper letters in the possession of Sir Ernst H. Gombrich which were made available to me on November 11, 1998 in the form of copies. Popper to Stebbing, April 28, 1943.
71 Popper Archives (305,13).
72 Quote from Stebbing in Popper Archives (300,2). Gombrich to Popper, July 11, 1943; quote from Hayek in 400,6. Hayek to Gombrich, June 28, 1943.
73 Prof. Stebbing was very ill at this time and no longer able to read the manuscript. Soon afterwards she had to undergo surgery. On September 17, 1943, Gombrich wrote to Popper, "You may have heard that Prof. Stebbing died last week, I never knew her but it seems to be a very real loss." (300,2). Popper replied on October 17th, "It was a great shock to hear that Stebbing has died. She was, to my knowledge, the only pupil of Russell's who had a chair in England."
74 On July 19, 1943, Popper commented on this, writing, "The cable nearly missed me. I got it only two days after it arrived in Christchurch, owing to the fact that my name was corrupted, or rather elevated, into 'Potter'!" (300,2)
75 Ibid. Gombrich to Popper, July 11, 1943. And on July 25 he adds, "I have just now finished your book and I find it in so many ways so marvellous that I would find it difficult and insulting to write you 'compliments' about it."
76 Popper Archives (305,13).
77 Popper Archives (300,2). Gombrich to Popper, July 28, 1943. The next Hayek quote found here as well.
78 And Gombrich wrote about Hayek, "You have really a very active and warm friend in Hayek, even beyond the matter of the book." (Ibid. Gombrich to Popper, August 21, 1943).
79 Ibid. Gombrich to Popper, August 11, 1943. Popper wrote to Gombrich on October 11, "Then came your kind airgraph of Aug. 21st, saying that the Syndici met on Sept. 24th. Seeing this, I began to hope again that a cable was on the way. But to-day, 17 days after the meeting, I feel that I must definitely abandon hope. If the outcome would have been positive, I should have got your cable at least a week ago. I confess that the impending decision made me incapable of writing to you; though I have worked most strenuously and successfully during this period on a paper on mathematical logic."
80 Popper Archives (300,2). Popper to Gombrich, August 23, 1943. Italics in original. The next quote found here as well.
81 Quoted in ibid., Gombrich to Popper, October 13, 1943. The next quotes found here as well. Popper comments on this in a November 22, 1943 letter to Gombrich, which reads as follows: "Regarding the quotation from H[ayek]'s letter, I still suspect that 'Plato' is only a euphemism of the three W's: Whitehead, Wittgenstein, Wisdom. I agree with H. that Cambridge's reasons are comic; but they are tragic as well; they must have been aware that the refusal may, in its effect, be equivalent to burning the book; and if they are so fond of the old philosopher king, they might have remembered from my book Kant's reply that philosophers should *not be debarred from being heard."* Gombrich responded on December 7th, "Personally I am not sure that you are right

there. And I wrote you before I think that you should really look on these tremendous difficulties as on a part of wartime difficulties. After all, the war here is still *very* near and the labour shortage makes itself felt in all aspects of life. Even books which are printed cannot be bound etc." (Italics in original).

82 Ibid. Gombrich to Popper, November 15, 1943. And later in this letter he goes on to add, "I don't feel that we should now show the MS. to other publishers, not even to other experts if we can help it. I feel that with Hayek, Laski and Levy it is beginning to be known to quite a sufficient number of 'bigwigs'."
83 Popper to Gombrich, November 22, 1943.
84 Ibid. Both quotes. Italics in original.
85 Popper to Gombrich, December 13, 1943, p. 2.
86 Popper Archives (300,3). Gombrich to Popper, January 5, 1944.
87 Popper to Gombrich, January 11, 1944. Later he continues, "Regarding the next steps to be taken, I have nothing whatever to add to my previous airgraphs. Only *one* thing: I do not think that it is worth waiting for a long time without attempting to force a decision." Italics in original.
88 Cf. also Fasz. 300,5. Hayek to Gombrich, January 14, 1944. My additions in [ ] are from Hayek's letter. Minor stylistic differences in Gombrich's quotation have not been changed.
89 Popper Archives (300,3). Gombrich to Popper, February 7, 1944. On February 14th, Gombrich sent a telegram to Popper which read: "Airmail arrived Hayek trying Routledge Ogden Series since Robbins failed us." Popper replied on February 15th: "I must say that the cable was the hardest blow so far; for with Macmillan, I really thought, for the first time that we will succeed, thanks to Hayek's and Robbins's influence."
90 Popper Archives (305,13). Popper to Hayek, March 14, 1944.
91 Popper Archives (300,3). And in a letter dated the same, he wrote, "By the way, I am sure you realize that I was rather unjust about Hayek in one of my last letters and that it was, in the end, he who placed the book."
92 At the end of this letter, Hennie Popper added an amusing account: "The cable was read over the telephone and I realized at once from K.'s answer that there was something happening. I was standing on a very wobby ladder in our spare room distempering the walls and swimming in 'Muresco'. I rushed to the telephone and kept looking over Karl's shoulder and under his arm while he was writing the message down, performing a silent 'Indian dance' and disturbing him greatly while the words came dripping down on the paper together with the Muresco. – It was the nicest Easter Monday I can remember, and I remember several quite nice ones in my former life. When I at last went back to my walls they had shrunk considerably and what had been before an endless expanse of dreary walls was suddenly a quite friendly looking little room which needed only a few strokes with a brush. So you see what miracles your cable has worked."
93 Popper Archives (28,2). Popper to Braunthal, August 23, 1943. He continued, "A publisher will show much more interest in a book if he is at once 'taken' by the title; for he judges that the public will react in a similar way as he does himself."
94 Popper Archives (28,6). Enclosure B, p. 2.

95 Ibid., p. 3. On May 21, 1943, Popper wrote to Alfred Braunthal, p. 2, "I have reason to believe that Macmillan's and Harper's rejections are due simply to the too provocative and too anti-Marxist title under which the book was offered to them ... I quite see that people don't want this sort of thing in these days, and they are right." Popper Archives (28,2).
96 Popper Archives (28,7). Italics in original. He goes on later to write, "This title-business is obviously important. Macmillan as well as Harper seem to have rejected the book without having read it, i.e. merely on account of the title. Thus the fate of the book may depend on such a thing."
97 Popper Archives (28,7). Hellin to Popper, May 22, 1943.
98 Popper Archives (28,2).
99 Popper letters in the possession of Sir Ernst H. Gombrich which were made available to me in the form of copies on June 26, 1998.
100 Popper Archives (300,2). Gombrich to Popper, November 15, 1943. Italics in original. And seven days later, before he could have received Gombrich's letter, Popper wrote, "Please tell me your opinions on the title-question. What do you think of "The Open Society and its Enemies" or of "A Social Philosophy for our Time", which latter title is of course, very pretentious." (November 22, 1943). On December 24, Popper responded to Gombrich's suggestions: "I think that 'Towards A Democratic Philosophy' comes into the narrow list; also 'From Plato to Marx: The Challenge to Democracy.' [I] – Concerning Table of Contents, etc. I now favour the following: Two parts only. I. The Open Society and Its Enemies. II. The Rise of Oracular Philosophy."
101 Popper Archives (305,13). Italics in original.
102 In John N. Findlay, "My Life: 1903-1973," in: *Studies in the Philosophy of J. N. Findlay*, ed. by Robert S. Cohen, Richard M. Martin, Merold Westphal, Albany: State University of New York Press, 1985, p. 26, Findlay claims that he convinced Popper *not* to give his book the title *False Prophets of History*. Apparently Findlay could no longer remember these events exactly when writing his biographical notes, for he also believed that Popper had gone to Christchurch as a *refugee* and that he had built the house in Cashmere himself. These assertions are just as incorrect as the title *False Prophets of History*, which Popper himself never mentioned. Watkins, "K. R. Popper", (see note 17), pp. 658-59, takes on this interpretation of the title question, and embroiders it, writing, "Findlay's widow claimed that he won Popper over to 'The Open Society'." (p. 659). On October 28, 1998, Alan Musgrave wrote me that it was Findlay "who suggested the title". The photo of Karl Popper and John Findlay has a notation on the back by Mrs Findlay which Watkins mentions. Mrs Findlay sent this photo to Robert S. Cohen at the Boston University with the following comment: "Dunedin, New Zealand 1944./ John Findlay and Karl Popper discussing Popper's manuscript of 'The Open Society'./ Popper wanted to call the book 'False Prophets of Society ... or Antiquity' but Findlay talked him out of that & suggested 'The Open Society'./ There are many humorous stories about the friendship of these two minds beleaguered in the wilds of New Zealand." (Written by Alan Musgrave on December 2, 1998). In contrast, Peter Munz wrote to me on

December 3, 1998, "The book was always referred to in the early forties in Christchurch as the Open Society."
103 Popper Archives (300,3).
104 Gombrich to Popper, March 17, 1944.
105 And he added, "I agree with the choice of 'The High Tide of Prophecy' as the sub-title of volume II; I suggest, however, either *not to add* any further remark (such as 'Hegel and Marx') or, if it must be, something like: '(Hegel, Marx, *and their Progeny*' or 'their Descendants' or 'their Offspring' (it does not matter if it sounds slightly ironical)." Etc. Italics in original.
106 Popper to Gombrich, April 22, 1944, p. 3.
107 Gombrich and Popper held different opinions about whether to divide the book before or after the Aristotle chapter. I do not wish to go into detail about this here, but would simply like to quote from a letter to Gombrich in which Popper explains the basis for his decision. "From the suggestion made to divide the book historically, i.e., into an ancient and a modern part, I realize that one tendency of the book has been mistaken. *The book was never intended as a historical survey of historicism.* It treats entirely and *exclusively problems of our own time,* and it attempts to shed some light upon them by showing that the character of some of these problems has been not properly understood so far. The problems treated are those of our civilization, that is to say, of certain ideas, and clashes of ideas; this forces me into a consideration of the history of certain relevant ideas. The result is, briefly: The Open Society creates, from the beginning, antagonism; every new move towards it is likely to create new antagonism. *These antagonisms are linked up with a historicist philosophy* . This historicist antagonism is particularly marked in two periods: That following the Great Generation, and that following the American and the French Revolution, down to our own day. – Thus the book divides into two parts: *1. Plato. 2. from Hegel to our own time.* Aristotle does not come in at all. He is, from the point of view of the book, nothing but the link between Plato and Hegel. As far as I and my book are concerned, he might have lived 300 or 1000 years after Plato. I need him, merely, because he is the more immediate source of Hegel's progressivist essentialism (teleology), and of Hegel's oracular cant. – Or to put it in another way. The book is on our own time, i.e., on Fascism and Marxism, and *therefore* on Plato and Hegel too. Aristotle plays the role of a 'preface to Hegel'. – This is how the book was planned, and why I recommend that, if a division into two volumes must be made, my original division 1. Plato. 2. Aristotle, Hegel, Marx, and followers – should be adhered to." Popper to Gombrich, April 14, 1944. Italics in Original.
108 Gombrich to Popper, June 10, 1944.
109 Cf. Malachi Haim Hacohen, "Karl Popper in Exile. The Viennese Progressive Imagination and the Making of *The Open Society,*" in: *Philosophy of the Social Sciences*, Vol. 26, Nr. 4, 1996, pp. 452-492. At the most, one could perhaps find a psychological component relevant in the case of Hennie Popper, who had a fear of large cities. She wrote to Gombrich on June 12, 1945, "I am frightfully scared by the prospect of going to London: I hate meeting new people, and the tea parties. I can only hope that tea is so rare

and precious that parties have gone out of fashion!" Popper letters in the possession of Sir Ernst H. Gombrich (see note 99).
110 Popper Archives (282,24). Popper to Carnap, June 23, 1945. On May 30th Carnap had inquired, "The news from Vienna are very interesting, but so far rather scarce. Would you ever consider any plans for returning there?, if a position were offered to you?"
111 Popper letters in the possession of Sir Ernst H. Gombrich (see note 99), no dates given.
112 Popper Archives (28,7). At almost the same time, he wrote to Gombrich, "Please excuse my nervousness which led to all these over-elaborate instructions and duplicated letters etc. It is due to the amazing and depressing experiences I had in my attempts to publish the book in U.S.A., and to the slow communication." Popper Archives (300,2). Popper to Gombrich, July 19, 1943.
113 Popper Archives (28,7). Italics in original. On the same day, Popper wrote to Braunthal, "It is now just a year that I sent the book to U.S.A. It took about 10 months before anybody read it. But, it appears, nobody (not even you) has so far done me the favour of reading my letters and instructions carefully; or if they did, they did not take any notice of them."October 12, 1943.
114 Popper Archives (28,2). Popper to Braunthal, October 12, 1943, pp. 2-3.
115 Popper Archives (300,2). Popper to Gombrich, July 22, 1943.
116 Popper to Gombrich, October 26, 1943. And on November 13th, after Gombrich had telegraphed him, "Hayek writes Nelson showed book enthusiastic Laski", Popper wrote, "I must indeed thank you for letting me have all cheering news in a depressing situation; it *has* cheered me up quite a lot, for I was depressed about Cambridge." (Italics in original).
117 Italics in original. On December 7th, Gombrich responded to the first quote, "I haven't at all given up hope to see the book published during the war but obviously the proposition is very different from what it would be in peacetime."
118 Popper to Gombrich, December 22, 1943.
119 Popper Archives (300,3).
120 Popper to Gombrich, September 4, 1944.
121 Popper Archives (300,4). Popper to Gombrich, March 28, 1945. Popper gives a somewhat different version of this account in a letter to Gombrich on April 9, 1945, where he added, "I am nearly 43 now, and if I don't manage to see you before I am 45, I may never have an opportunity: I don't think that anybody would import to England a lecturer over the age of 45". On April 11, 1945, he wrote to Hayek concerning the book's release, "I had naively expected that it would come out by December 1944: Gombrich had written, after the conference with Mr. Read on March 17, 1944, that Mr. Read offers to start setting up at once, and that he expected the first volume to take nine months. Mr. Read himself wrote to me later that they decided to publish both vols. at the same time and that this procedure would not hold up the publication of vol. I ..." (305,13).
122 Popper Archives (300,3). Italics in original.

123 Gombrich to Popper, March 17, 1944. On April 12, 1945, Gombrich told Popper what he had spent in the meantime on proof-reading, the preparation of indices, and the application for the LSE post: "This, if I am right, is 28 guineas or 29 £ 8 shillings, and may it be the last expense into which I have to drag you. I have a bad conscience to have to distribute ducats like this on your behalf, but there it is." (300,4)
124 Popper Archives (300,3). Popper had written to him on April 22nd, "So please, try to find somebody reliable for reading the proofs etc. (against payment) and *don't do it yourself.*" Italics in original.
125 Popper Archives (28,3).
126 Popper letters in the possession of Sir Ernst H. Gombrich (see note 99).
127 Popper Archives (300,3). Popper to Gombrich, September 4, 1944.
128 Popper to Gombrich, September 12, 1944. In this letter, Popper gives detailed reasons for the corrections.
129 Popper Archives (300,4). Popper to Gombrich, January 25, 1945. Popper was of the opinion, "How you should proceed in case R. does indeed intend to postpone publication, I have no idea. I think you might consult a lawyer, preferably Kilham Roberts, the lawyer of the author's society; in any case you might tell them that such a step would shake my confidence in them – especially since they did not inform us at once." In the hand-written original, the last *us* is in italics. Cf. Popper letters in the possession of Sir Ernst H. Gombrich (see note 99), January 24, 1945, p. 5.
130 Popper Archives (300,4). Gombrich to Popper, January 15, 1945.
131 Quoted in ibid., Gombrich to Popper, February 8, 1945.
132 Italics in original.
133 Gombrich to Popper, February 20, 1945.
134 On March 28, 1945, Popper answered, "I am terribly sorry that my impatience concerning the publication date has called forth such thoughts [namely that Gombrich had taken part of the responsibility for the delays upon himself, H.K.] in you, and my only comfort is that I can use this opportunity to tell you again what your friendship and help has meant to me in an otherwise rather terrible time."
135 Popper letters in the possession of Sir Ernst H. Gombrich (see note 99). Italics in original. To Gombrich, he added by hand, "I hope you won't find this letter too strong. That it will hardly help, I know, of course, myself. But I should very much like to hear whether you found it too bad." On July 24, 1945, Gombrich answered, "I think your letter to Read wasn't at all too sharp". Popper Archives (300,4).
136 300,4. Gombrich to Popper, July 5, 1945.
137 Quoted from ibid., Popper to Gombrich, August 25, 1945. Next quote also found here.
138 Popper Archives (305,13).
139 Popper letters in the possession of Sir Ernst H. Gombrich (see note 99). Popper to Gombrich, November 14, 1945.
140 Cf. Frederick A. Hayek, *The Road to Serfdom,* London: Routledge, 1944, 1976.
141 Popper Archives (300,3). Popper to Gombrich, September 4, 1944, p. 2. A detailed discussion of these doubts of Popper's is not presented here. It is

sufficient to quote the following excerpt from a letter in order to clarify why Popper did not want to be connected with Hayek's book. "I hope the publisher will accept this addition without making any objection; but if he objects, then please tell him that there are certain striking similarities between my book and Prof. Hayek's *Road to Serfdom*... Now I should not mind, of course, to be considered as under the influence of this excellent book; but the fact is that I was independent. But my main point is that I do not wish that anybody who notices these similarities (and the great success of Prof. Hayek's book makes it probable that some will notice them) should think that I have used Prof. Hayek's ideas *without acknowledgement*. This would be very bad indeed ... but as matters are, such a reference to his book would look like a claim to fame, a claim to participate in his success, which of course would be quite ridiculous since there are very many and very important things said in his book of which there is no trace in mine; for in spite of the similarities mentioned, the books are, of course, very different indeed." Popper to Gombrich, June 5, 1944, p. 2. Italics in original.

142 Popper Archives (305,13).
143 Cf. ibid., Popper to Hayek, December 8, 1943, where Popper wrote, "I have sent you at once a cable 'Should like to be considered'. There is no doubt in my mind that it must be a wonderful thing to be able to work in the L.S.E. and that the post you describe in your kind letter must be ideal; I am thinking especially of the work with research students, and of the prospect to continue my work on the methodology of the social sciences."
144 Popper Archives (400,6).
145 Popper Archives (300,2). The next two quotes also found here. Italics in original. Likewise, the application materials can be found here. I find Popper's description of his university studies particularly interesting and worth quoting:
"University Studies: I studied, at the University of Vienna, at first mathematics and physics. Encouraged by my teacher, Prof. H. Hahn, to read Principia Mathematica, my interests were decidedly turned towards the problem of the rational foundation of science. Since then, nearly all my studies have been devoted to this problem. I soon started to study philosophy, specializing in epistemology and the theory of scientific method. My teachers in Philosophy were Professors Schlick, Gomperz, and Bühler. For my examination as a secondary school teacher in mathematics and physics, I wrote a thesis on the foundations of geometry ('Axiome, Postulate und Definitionen der Geometrie'). My philosophical interests centered in an attempt to compare the methods of the natural sciences with those of the social sciences and of psychology. This determined the subject of my doctor's thesis which was devoted to an analysis of the methods of the psychology of thinking ('Zur Methodenfrage der Denkpsychologie'). In 1928, I passed with 'Einstimmig mit Auszeichnung' (corresponding to First Class Honours) my *rigorosa* or final examinations for the Doctor's degree in Philosophy." (Ibid., p. 2, Italics in original).
146 Popper Archives (305,13). Later Hayek added, "So, I am afraid, however unpleasant that must be, you will have to resign yourself to a perhaps pro-

longed period of uncertainty with the possibility of a very sudden decision in the end."
147 Popper Archives (300,2). In contrast, Hayek wrote to Gombrich on October 29, 1943, concerning the publication of the book by Nelsons and the LSE position, "it will be a tremendous help in connection with my other plans, which, if they come off, may be of even greater importance for Dr. Popper than whether his book is accepted by any particular publisher" (305,13). On January 11, 1944, Popper wrote to Gombrich: "I should, of course, love to go to England as soon as possible, and not merely after the war." (300,3)
148 The circumstances surrounding the internal decision are presented by Watkins, "K. R. Popper", (see note 17), pp. 659-60, based on LSE files. Cf. also David Miller, "Sir Karl Raimund Popper, C.H., F.B.A. 28. Juli 1902-17. September 1994," in: *Biogr. Mems Fell. R.S. Lond.*, Vol. 43, 1997, p. 380.
149 Popper Archives (300,3). Gombrich to Popper, January 16, 1944.
150 Gombrich to Popper, February 29, 1944. Italics in original.
151 Popper Archives (300,4). Gombrich to Popper, January 15, 1945.
152 Detailed description in Popper Archives (305,13). Popper to Hayek, October 23, 1944.
153 Popper Archives (300,3). On January 26, 1945, Popper wrote to Gombrich, "Concerning the Perth chair, I must say first that my chances that they will offer me this chair are *extremely* slender; but they are not nil, and in case I should get this offer, it is probable that this will occur *before* the London decision will be made; for they probably want the new professor to take up duties as soon as possible, and the academic year begins in March. The Perth chair would be a much better position than the Dunedin one – for many reasons (although my chances in Dunedin would be better; but Dunedin is not yet advertised). I could not afford declining Perth for an uncertain possibility in the L.S.E., much as I should prefer the L.S.E. position *if I had a choice*. But the point is that in all likelihood, I shall have no choice, owing to the fact that L.S.E. will probably be decided much later.
But I should like *not to withdraw my application* from the L.S.E., and to attempt to make some arrangement with Perth should the L.S.E. appointment come after the Perth appointment. My plans are as follows: If I get Perth, I intend to cable to you and to Prof. Hayek; if you get such a cable, then please send Prof. Hayek this letter. In my cable to Prof. Hayek, I intend to stress my preference for London and the need for accepting Perth if the London decision has not been made; at the same time, I would say that I do not wish to withdraw my application for the L.S.E. since an arrangement with Perth might be reached." (300,4. Italics in original).
154 Popper Archives (300,4). Popper to Gombrich, February 10, 1945, upon which Gombrich replied, "It would be lovely to lecture to Koalas, I am sure." Gombrich to Popper, April 12, 1945. Popper refused the offer from Sydney twice!
155 Here also the quote about the salary. Gombrich explained, "After deduction of taxes and addition of allowances I get some £ 40 a month of which I pay £ 15 for our flat. Food costs little (because it's rationed) but all 'extras' like laundry, doctors, coal, travel etc. cost a tremendous lot."
156 Popper Archives (400,6). Hayek to Gombrich, January 8, 1945.

157 Popper Archives (300,4).
158 Cf. Popper Archives (305,13). Hayek to Popper, March 19, 1945.
159 Popper Archives (300,4).
160 And on April 9th, he added, "What you say about Hayek's departure is very true – it will certainly have a bad effect."
161 Gombrich to Popper, April 12, 1945.
162 Popper Archives (305,13).
163 Popper Archives (300,4). Popper to Gombrich, May 4, 1945. Italics in original.
164 Karl R. Popper, "Towards an Evolutionary Theory of Knowledge," in, by the same: *A World of Propensities,* Bristol: Thoemmes, 1990, p. 29.
Nevertheless, I would like to quote from Popper's personal account to his friend Gombrich, dated June 12, 1945, because it is more authentic: "But I must tell you what happened here. During the whole of April I was ill again. I am now always getting such terrible colds – starting with a very sore throat, and developing in all directions. I was very weak. My doctor insisted that I should go to the mountains during the May vacations and we both went to the Hermitage, at the foot of Mt Cook (the highest mountain here). I was first pretty miserable there, but after two days I had a marvellous recovery; we went up to a hut (the Ball Hut – see pictures in 'Mt. Cook and the Glaciers') where we were very happy. On the bus journey back from the Hermitage, on May 21st, in the first village, called Fairlie, the Postmistress came with a cable to the bus. It was addressed to 'Karl Popper c/o Bus from Hermitage to Fairlie' and said 'Congratulations on London appointment and thanks for excellent article enquiring about permits Frederick Hayek'. It was from Cambridge, May 16th. This was the first we heard about it. I had given up the idea of going to London – though sub-consciously I still believed in it." Popper Archives (300,4).
165 Later we read, "I am now going to tell them [the publisher, H.K.] of your appointment, may be it will 'ginger them up', it is, of course, a good thing also for your book since there is bound to be interest in the L.S.E. circles what kind of a bird you will turn out to be."
166 Popper Archives (305,13).
167 Popper Archives (300,2). Popper to Gombrich, December 22, 1943. Italics in original.
168 Popper Archives (305,13).
169 Popper Archives (300,4). Italics in original.
170 Popper Archives (305,13). Cf. also Popper to Hayek, August 8, 1945. In this letter we also read, "Yesterday we heard about the atomic bomb. I am appalled at the possible social repercussions of the harness of atomic energy. It may easily mean the end of free research – of science – and of all freedom. I am very sorry for Niels Bohr, one of the greatest and best men alive."
171 Popper Archives (300,4). Popper to Gombrich, August 25, 1945.
172 Popper Archives (305,13).
173 Popper to Hayek, September 8, 1945.
174 Popper letters in the possession of Sir Ernst H. Gombrich (see note 99). Italics in original.
175 Ibid. Popper to Gombrich, November 16, 1945.

176 Peter Munz kindly informed me of the exact date on December 4, 1998. On November 21, 1945, he had received a letter from Karl Popper posted from Auckland, in which he mentions this departure date.
177 Gombrich, *The Open Society and Its Enemies,* (see note 3), p. 16. Colin Simkin, *Popper's Views on Natural and Social Science,* Leiden, New York, Cologne: Brill, 1993, p. 189, writes: "After eight years of comparative obscurity in a small and distant university college, Karl became almost immediately famous in a great intellectual centre, where he stayed for the rest of his salaried career."
178 Popper Archives (300,4). Italics in original.
179 Popper Archives (29, 5-6). Barker was most hurt by Popper's "demolishing Plato's spell" and his attacks on the king of philosophy. "Why, in particular, the sad but ruthless onslaught on the genius of Plato?" All the other reviews which I quote may be found in this 29, 5-6.
180 Cf. W. J. Gardner, E. T. Beardsley, T. E. Carter, *A History of the University of Canterbury* 1873-1973, Christchurch: University of Canterbury, 1973, p. 308.
181 Quoted in Popper Archives (28,2). Popper to Braunthal, November 2, 1943.
182 Popper Archives (282,24).

Popper's "Negative Utilitarianism"
From Utopia to Reality

Erich Kadlec

I.

In "The Open Society and Its Enemies" Karl Popper formulated the, in his opinion, most important principles of a humanitarian form of ethics attributing equal rights to all human beings (vol.1, chapter 5, note 6):

(1) Tolerance towards all who are not intolerant and who do not propagate intolerance.
(2) The recognition that all moral urgency has its basis in the urgency of suffering or pain.
(3) The fight against tyranny; the attempt to safeguard the other principles by the institutional means of legislation rather than the benevolence of persons in power.

From item (2) Popper derives the proposition to replace the utilitarian formula "Maximize happiness" by the formula "Minimize suffering". He believes that such a simple formula can be one of the fundamental principles (admittedly not the only one) of public policy. In contrast he considers the principle "Maximize happiness" as apt to produce a benevolent dictatorship. We should realise that, from the moral point of view suffering and happiness must not be treated as symmetrical; the promotion of happiness is in any case less urgent than the rendering of help to those who suffer, and the attempt to prevent suffering. The latter task has little to do with "matters of taste", the former very much (vol. I, chapter 5, note 6, para 2).

Popper judges from the ethical point of view both the Utilitarian principle "Maximize happiness" and Kant´s principle "Promote the other people's happiness..." as wrong. This, however, is not completely decidable by rational argument (vol. I, chapter 9, note 2).

In Popper's opinion human suffering makes a direct moral appeal, namely the appeal for help while there is no similar call to increase the happiness of a human being who is doing well anyway (vol. I, chapter 9; note 2).

A further criticism of the Utilitarian formula "Maximize happiness" is that it allows us to treat degrees of pain as negative degrees of pleasure. From the moral point of view, however, pain cannot be offset by pleasure, and especially not one person's pain by another person's pleasure. Instead of asking for the greatest happiness for the greatest number one should demand, more modestly, the least amount of avoidable suffering for all; and further, that unavoidable suffering – such as hunger in times of an unavoidable shortage of food – should be distributed as equally as possible. Popper furthermore visualises some analogy between this view of ethics and his view of scientific methodology, advocated in his "The Logic of Scientific Discovery" (1935). It adds to clarity in the field of ethics if we formulate our demands negatively – the elimination of suffering rather than the promotion of happiness. Similarly, it is helpful to formulate the task of a scientific method as the elimination of false theories rather than the attainment of established truths (vol. I, chapter 9, note 2).

Popper concludes his "The Open Society and Its Enemies" by committing himself to the principle of man's autonomy and asks for the defence and strengthening of democratic institutions as prerequisites of freedom and progress. Progress rests with us, with our watchfulness, with our efforts, with the clarity of our conception of our ends, and with the realism of their choice (vol. II, chapter 25). This "realism of the choice means we should choose ends which can be realised within a reasonable span of time and should avoid distant and vague utopian ideals (vol. II, chapter 25, note 28).

In 1961 Popper wrote an addendum I to volume II: "Facts, Standards and Truth, a further criticism of relativism" in which he summarises his thoughts on the dualism of facts and moral standards and compares the search for essential standards with the search for truth as postulated by Tarski. The regulatory idea of absolute "correctness" or "benevolence" in its logical status differs from that of an absolute truth (vol. II: Addendum I/13). We create our standards by proposing, discussing and accepting them. The idea of truth may, nevertheless, also be used as a kind of model for standards. We may look for absolutely correct or valid proposals – or at least for better or more valid ones. There can be no criterion for absolute correctness, however – and the less so for absolute truth (vol. II: Addendum I/13).

This brings Popper back to Utilitarianism. "Maximize happiness" was once seen as a criterion. Popper's proposition "Minimize suffering" had never been meant as a criterion (although this upgrades some of the ideas inherent in Utilitarianism). Popper refers to his recommendation to consider minimizing avoidable suffering as a task of public policy while maximizing happiness should be undertaken privately. Although we do not have a criterion for absolute moral correctness, we may – just as in the field of facts – very well encounter progress and discoveries: cruelty is always "evil" and should by all means be avoided, the "Golden Rule" is a good standard which might even be improved by treating others wherever possible the way they would wish themselves to be treated and[1], by applying Socrates´ axiom that you had better suffer injustice than inflict it. All the above activities are elementary and essential examples of discoveries in the field of moral standards (vol. II, Addendum I/13).

II.

However much Popper's activities influenced politicians in the second half of the 20th Century in actual practice his theory of a "negative" Utilitarianism met with little echo in scientific circles. The academia paid little attention, reacted with rejection and a lack of understanding. Critics hardly dealt with the subject matter of the theory and did not grasp the importance of a universal competence of conflict settlement Popper's ideas had offered and which had not existed in CU (Classical Utilitarianism) before.

1. R.N. Smart (in "Mind", 1958, vol.67)

names Popper's suggestion "Negative Utilitarianism" (henceforth NU) and attempts to lead it ad absurdum by drafting the theoretical experiment of a "benevolent destroyer of the universe", vested with the power of a painless annihilation of humankind and according to the rules of NU obliged to put an end to all suffering by exterminating all human beings (and all animals).

Although Smart himself has doubts about this line of thought and is aware from the point of view of positive Utilitarianism that this would extinguish also all joy and happiness of human beings, he insinuates that NU would require that from the claim for minimizing suffering also the claim for exterminating humankind, killing and abortion be deduced. He compares the painlessness of being quickly killed with the greater pain of toothache and concludes that pity with the victim is irrational. Followers of NU would have to regard death as divine bliss the way religious people do.

Smart sees the only advantage of NU as a political principle in the likelihood of agreement among human beings on what is evil than on what is good. But this clarification is purchased at the price of "absurd" or even "evil" moral judgments.

The two other principles Popper links with NU, i.e. "Tolerance towards the tolerant" and "No tyranny" also fail to stop Smart from refusing NU. Even if these principles supported NU there would be conflicting interests between the latter and NU as regards Smart`s example. Would the benevolent destroyer of the universe be the saviour of humankind and animals, Smart asks as a rhetoric question and concludes his criticism with the sarcastic comment that the devoted protagonist of NU might see a new meaning in the connotation: "Whom the Gods love die young".

Smart`s refusal of NU is based on a conclusion as premise, in no way explained by him, on his arbitrary assumption of an "obligation", deduced from the principle of minimizing suffering, to kill all (suffering) people for the sake of eliminating their pain. By postulating this obligation of a fictitious benevolent destroyer of the universe – as such a contradictio in adjecto – vis-à-vis all humankind (and all animals) he contradicts his very own assertion that also happy people fall victims to his radicalism. He also dispenses with the generally known fact that all people (with a few exceptions in extreme situations) like to live and would consider being killed not as a benefit but as the greatest evil done to them. This highhanded pretension of a disposability of other people's lives, or even an elimination of the entire evolutionary input in the development of humankind vehemently contradicts Popper's ideology and discredits something Popper never maintained.

Smart uses the term "eliminating" where Popper speaks of "minimizing", thus contradicting his own quotation of Popper's "the smallest scale of avoidable pain for all" (OS I, chapter 9, note 2), which presupposes the continued existence of people who feel joy and pain. Just as Note 6 to chapter 5 in vol. I, cited by Smart himself, where "help for the suffering" is distinguished from "the attempt to avoid suffering", shows that Popper's NU defies the very creation of suffering and wishes to mitigate existing pain – exactly the opposite of Smart`s confusion of the elimination of mankind with the elimination of their suffering.

Smart`s argumentation, although in contrast to all rules of logic, becomes the subject of serious discussions, marginalising Popper's proposition.

2. J.J.C Smart (in "An Outline of a System of Utilitarian Ethics", Melbourne 1961)

sides with the before-mentioned opinion of his brother and has doubts as to a propagation of NU. He only accepts it as an inferior rule of thumb, that it is actually easier to minimize human suffering than to provide tangible happiness.

3. H.B. Acton (in "Aristotelian Society, 1963, Supplement, Vol. 37: 83-94)

concentrates on Smart's rejection and would agree with him if the elimination of suffering were the only principle of NU. But to eliminate suffering is, as Acton states, not the same as to reduce suffering "to the smallest scale of avoidable suffering" (Popper loc cit.) which might perhaps serve as a replacement for the positive form of Utilitarianism. Would a destroyer of the universe inspired by Smart not commit a terrible mistake by not recognising the difference between "eliminate" and "reduce"?

Acton deals with Popper's three principles in their context and is primarily interested in Popper's perception of the asymmetry of suffering and joy and the greater urgency of the moral plea to help people in distress rather than to provide joy for those not in distress. He considers Popper's remark that this differentiation is an emotional action and not a "subject for rational argument" as not sufficient and asks for further investigations in order to obtain further knowledge on the structure of ethics, in particular compassion ethics (he also refers to Schopenhauer's "Two Fundamental Problems of Ethics"). The different kinds of suffering, methods and forms of help and the person of the helper should be investigated.

Acton differentiates between 1. suffering caused by illness or accident and 2. pain caused by third parties, such as violation, the frustration of prisoners and mortification, and 3. self- induced suffering. He combines the cause of suffering with the urgency of the plea for help. Since increasing happiness of a happy person might be more urgent than helping a person responsible him/herself for suffering, Acton, in contrast to Popper, cannot discern a principle of priority of helping those suffering over promoting happiness although he readily admits the priority of help for groups 1 and 2 and also acknowledges that causing pain by third parties (group 2) will always be morally wrong.

As regards the forms of help he commences by dealing with helping oneself by employing the respective experts such as e.g. physicians whom the afflicted person helps to earn a living by paying a fee – in which case the moral aspect lies in the interest of the person concerned. In other cases a suffering person has to rely on third party help but the person who could help refrains from doing so because he or she enjoys seeing the other one suffer or is not interested. Where people behave in this way there is no reason why they should not (be considered to) inflict pain themselves if they enjoy doing this or benefit from it? For a person not ready to help others when in need there is no reason for not hurting others if this brings an advantage. In this way hurting and not helping coincide.

By putting active hurting on the same level as passive failure to act helpfully, an unrealistic approach contradictory to all practical (penal law) systems applied, Acton obstructs access to Popper's claim for "preventing suffering" (vol. I, chapter 5, note 6, para 2), i.e. not to inflict pain on the one hand and hinder others to do so on the other. He therefore only deals with the aspect of rendering help without referring to the obligation of preventing assaults by third parties.

Acton finally considers it quite possible that rational reasons could be found for the negative principle: People in distress are more likely to require help. He postulates this as dependent on the cause of their condition, however. This should lead to the realisation that a difference must be made between hurting and helping, since hurting demonstrates a lack of interest in others while helping is evidence of greater interest in oneself. This differentiation does not imply consequences in the form of an inhibition to hurt, however, as Popper sees it as a prevention of the creation of suffering (vol. I, chapter 5, note 6, para 2). Acton thus ignores that NU over and above the Utilitarian principle gains a new dimension of the competence of conflict settlement as a result of the demand to prevent suffering that inherently includes the prohibition to inflict pain.

Acton summarily acknowledges that concern for suffering beings necessitates more urgent help since an injury is more important then mere damage. Pain and suffering are connected with injury and destruction, happiness, on the other hand, is connected with success. It would be fatal to promote success without securing survival. Pain damages the entire life, failure to succeed does not. A person caring for others will, of necessity, be morally more engaged if another being suffers. According to Acton this does not imply that it is morally more important to help in such a situation. The different aspects of the two situations are explained by Acton by referring to a question he borrowed from J. Bentham: whether poetry or sanitary installations are more important (in Bentham's text simple toys)!

4. J.W.N.Watkins (in "Aristotelian Society, 1963, Supplement, vol. 37:95-114),

Popper's successor at LSE, published his article as Part Two of H.B. Acton's contribution under the subject heading of NU but does not deal with Popper's theory and explicitly mentions this. He refers to himself as a negative Utilitarian who is anti-evil rather than pro-good and considers his attitude as part of a comprehensive moral negativism.

His comment on Popper's theory is limited to the remark that Acton exceeds in partially agreeing with Smart since Popper did not really stipulate what Acton blames him for. Watkins agrees with Acton that arguments over conflicting moral principles are quite possible. While Acton approaches the problem in "bottom-up" style investigating the different kinds of suffering and help, Watkins embarks on the opposite journey and investigates "top-down" whether ethic principles and moral policy should be subjected to criticism at all. His approach is based on his – not further explained – conviction of the scientific autonomy of ethics and his dismissal of Kant's apriorism and of naturalism in general. By referring to Popper's "The Logic of Scientific Discovery" he endeavours to establish a theory of rational argumentation, elaborating an analogy of explanatory requirements to those in natural sciences, hoping to obtain the same result as Acton. Although he generally asserts that morality is a question of behaviour vis-à-vis others, that ethics should offer the competence of conflict settlement and ethic subjectivism should be avoided, he fails to examine Popper's draft for evidence in how far the requirements postulated by him are met with in NU, in particular by the claim for preventing the creation of pain with the inherent prohibition to inflict pain.

5. A.D.M. Walker (in "Mind", 1974, vol. 83:424-28)

does not deal with Popper's theory either, the latter not even being mentioned, but with Acton's article written in 1963. His criticism of classical (positive) Utilitarianism attacks the principle of utmost happiness (Mill), the obviously equal treatment of joy and pain, of mitigating or preventing suffering and of promoting happiness. He considers Acton's opinion of the moralistic asymmetry (as shown by Popper) as too restricted as he is only concerned with existing pain and the creation of future happiness. Furthermore, he points towards further asymmetries in terms of time, such as the promotion of future happiness of A if this implies future pain for B, attributing priority to the prevention of suffering (all this on condition of equal preconditions and consequences). Walker voices doubts, though: if the mitigation of A`s pain were obtained at the expense of B`s happiness, this would curtail B`s vested rights. As regards the kind of asymmetry between the infliction of pain and the failure to help, Walker supports Ross's view (Foundation of Ethics) as not exaggerated, when he states that inflicting pain is justified if this entails not an equivalent but a substantially higher degree of happiness for somebody else – exactly the opposite of Popper's view of categorically excluding the idea that the suffering of one person is offset by the happiness of another.

A further asymmetry not paid attention to in CU must be seen in the severity of the obligation to help and to eliminate inflicting pain on the one hand and the obligation to promote happiness and prevent any failure to achieve this on the other. In this context Walker also refers to K.E. Tranöy (Asymmetries in Ethics, Inquiry 1967) and arrives at the conclusion that inflicting pain should always be avoided and that pain should be mitigated whenever this is possible. A similar obligation to provide joy for others would appear to be less obvious. To help and not to inflict pain is seen as a matter of course. Failure to render help or not prevent the infliction of pain should be seen as much more objectionable than any failure in the promotion of happiness.

A further group of asymmetries is discovered by Walker in the exceptions from moral rules. The effort required for keeping a promise and the delight when breaking it in no way justify not keeping it. One would expect from CU to consider such delight and forms of pain as equivalent. When taking into account special circumstances some revisions would be necessary, however.

Modifying CU is required with regard to the asymmetries. Walker suggests doing this in the form of an amendment which he calls NU, i.e. to evaluate joy and pain differently and attribute more importance to pain than to diminishing joy. He opines, however, that it is not necessary to discard CU, nor to acknowledge NU as a separate, not derived moral principle. Walker undertakes several adaptation attempts, none of which strikes him as convincible. He eventually arrives at a principle of fair distribution of happiness as an amendment to CU and maintains that this addition renders NU unnecessary as an independent principle. The respective modifications of CU would lead to radical changes of Utilitarianism compared with its original concept. The asymmetries referred to are not limited to the field of ethics but may crop up everywhere in the life of human beings: we use standards for expressing what is sufficiently satisfactory or at least acceptable. Where this minimum standard is not reached, we refer to a deficiency, a shortage, etc.; to help those who do not reach the standard is considered more urgent and has a higher value than to support those who already live in satisfactory conditions.

In admitting this Walker has entered the conceptual sphere of NU, even if he rejects it formally and attempts sticking to positive Utilitarianism. In order to document this insistence he uses the example of a mechanic repairing a broken down engine instead of exchanging the defective parts for new ones. Since Walker never dealt with Popper's proposition he did not realise that his claim for a competence of conflict settlement of a moral principle had already been met by Popper's claim for preventing pain (vol. 1, chapter 5, note 6, para 2), with its inherent primary inhibition to inflict pain, an axiom not achieved in CU with its hedonistic calculus of outbalancing joy and pain of the different persons "concerned".

6. S. Pralong (in "Popper's Open Society after 50 Years", Routledge London and New York 1999)

In her article "Is there An Ethics in the Open Society" examines Popper's contribution half a century after its publication for implicitly contained criteria of minimum ethics in the individual behaviour towards other human beings. She bases her findings not only on Popper's NU of minimizing suffering which he suggests as basis for public policy but also on Popper's moral standards as outlined above all in his addendum I to volume II.

Contrary to J. Shearmur (The Political Thought of Karl Popper, Routledge London and New York 1996) who accuses Popper of neglecting the differences between public and private obligations and, consequently, of not meeting the responsibility vis-à-vis the other human being, Pralong does not regard this as a failure of his since these obligations represent a moral continuum in both areas and since, according to NU, the same procedural standards apply to public policy and to the solution of private moral dilemmas. For Pralong the formula "Minimize suffering" is a token of a specific method of moral argumentation which can be used in the same way in private as in public.

In her interpretation of the Open Society Pralong joins forces with Shearmur's view of a kind of ethic objectivism on the part of Popper, with methodological analogies towards his theory of science (Shearmur loc cit.). She supports her view by quoting Popper a number of times, primarily on the autonomy of the individual in his or her moral decision as basis for his or her responsibility. Irrespective of Popper's negation of an absolute moral criterion she offers approaches for an extension of NU's ideas as a guideline for private action. She quotes Popper's remarks on Kant and his categorical imperative and his deliberations on the Golden Rule as an example of a moral standard he wants to see further improved by stipulating that other people should possibly be treated the way they themselves wish to be treated (OS, vol. II, Addendum I/13).

Although this quotation points towards the positive formula of the Golden Rule since the expectations of those concerned comprise both avoiding suffering and providing help, Pralong arguments in the opposite direction and concentrates on interpreting the negative formulation of the Golden Rule "We shouldn't do to others what we wouldn't want others to do unto us" as an ethic norm that is simple to follow and is applicable in private as well as in public life. By expressing the Golden Rule in the negative formula Pralong believes to avoid any imputation of one's own standards which would entail the danger of subjectivism and relativism since the unwanted suffering that should be avoided is seen on more common terms by humankind than happiness. Her idea, in turn, offers the possibility of universalising the moral principle.

However much these thoughts should meet with approval an essential component of the idea of NU remains unaccomplished by merely formulating the Golden Rule in the negative: minimizing suffering by acting in the case of existing (or imminent) suffering. Pralong thus misses the chance of comparing NU with CU and demonstrating the superiority of NU resulting from the asymmetry of utmost urgency of the moral ban to inflict pain ahead of the obligation to mitigate existing pain by helping. Popper's NU comprises both principles and the inhibition of any detrimental action – according to Pralong the sole content of the moral principle raised by her – includes a further competence, i.e. the settlement of conflicting interests between those acting and those concerned.

III. Summary:

1. Popper's proposition of the so-called "Negative Utilitarianism" containing the principle "Minimize suffering" was not intended as the sole criterion of absolute rightness but as an improvement upgrading some of the ideas inherent in Classical Utilitarianism ("Maximize happiness"), intended to be applied in public policy. In the field of social politics NU offers a number of advantages over CU:
1.1. The central concept of NU's "suffering" represents an internal sensation of humankind in the same way CU's claim for "happiness" does. While happiness as a fulfilment of subjective and intrinsically diverging aspirations of individual people a priori jeopardises any general rule and it cannot be predicted what will make a person happy, the creation of suffering will prove attributable to essentially the same causes. Everyone knows which events cause pain while no one can reliably predict measures to ensure general happiness. A policy aiming at minimizing suffering offers more precise aspects than one addressing maximum happiness.
1.2. Popper's elaborated asymmetry of the urgency of the claim for minimizing or preventing suffering as a priority over the invitation to increase happiness is evident and is in no way disputed by his critics. In comparison, the hedonistic calculus of CU with its quantification of happiness and pain not only permits but even calls for accumulating larger quantities of happiness at the expense of smaller quantities of pain irrespective of the persons concerned, i.e. happiness of one person at the expense of the other one, and disrupts the moral asymmetry as conceived by Popper.
1.3. In line with his humanistic ideology Popper objects to pain being caused for the benefit of increasing happiness, in particular where the happiness of one person is purchased by the suffering of the other one. His individualistic NU, directed at the protection of the individual against the arbitrariness of a third party, takes moral priority over the collectivistic CU aiming at maximum happiness for a maximum of persons.
1.4. NU avoids the internal contradiction of CU to endeavour basing the collectivistic principle on fulfilling a maximum number of as such diverging and not consistent wishful ideas of individuals. This CU-inherent contradiction hosts a germ for misunderstanding and involuntarily foisted happiness. Since every human being strives to obtain a fairly individual happiness, it does not make sense to perceive this

overall aspiration as the basis of a moral system. It is the very egoism of the individual's strife for happiness which causes the problems moral principles and standards serve to regulate.

1.5. The "certain analogy" between NU's guidelines stipulating realism and modesty as described by Popper and his scientific methodology according to "The Logic of Scientific Discovery" essentially contribute towards better clarity in the field of ethics as a result of the negative formulation of the claims (see also 2.1. and 2.2. below).

1.6. Popper's postulate of a realistic setting of ends is realised in NU. Preventing and eliminating suffering is a concrete, achievable task, accomplished the moment pain is not caused or has been eliminated. Happiness achieved by means of satisfying individual desires is subject to a habituation process, ever and again creating new dissatisfaction and new desires which in the long run cannot be realised.

1.7. The realistic modesty of NU is faced with the utopian ideal of the promise of general happiness in CU, running the risk of becoming a very dangerous kind of benevolent dictatorship with unrealisable promises. The 20th Century has furnished ample proof that Popper was right in his misgivings in this field.

1.8. NU offers the better solution also as regards costs. The public means required for minimizing suffering require much smaller funds than the never ending task of bringing about overall happiness which can only be aimed at by an indirect excessive allocation of goods.

2. In his Addendum I to Volume II (1961) Popper, in an explanation of his reasoning when writing his contribution, supplemented his proposition of an improved Utilitarianism over and above the sphere of application of social pragmatism with the moral standards, listed by him in exemplary fashion such as that cruelty is always "evil", that the Golden Rule is a good standard (which could perhaps be further improved), and included in the 1992 German edition („ Tatsachen, Maßstäbe und Wahrheit, eine weitere Kritik des Relativismus") revised by Popper himself, Socrates´ realisation that one should rather suffer injustice than inflict it. This has opened a new dimension of NU, i.e. the dimension of a moral standard for the correctness of the personal behaviour of human beings in relation to others:

2.1. The first asymmetry of the priority of minimizing suffering of NU over maximizing happiness of CU is extended by a second one, partly not acknowledged by the supporters of CU, partly denied (H.B. Acton), the asymmetry inherent in Popper's formula: his claim for avoiding suffering implies – and this as a priority – the demand of oneself not to inflict suffering on someone else.

2.2. The negatively formulated moral principles, i.e. to refrain from certain actions (such as Decalogue, Golden Rule) generally demonstrate more importance far beyond the field of Utilitarianism than the positive invitation to become helpfully active. Practical (legal) systems, too, correspond to the priority of the prohibition of certain actions over the obligation to perform certain activities and declare extremely reprehensible acts punishable while failure to act helpfully (with the exception of an infringement of specific obligations to help such in the case of physicians, responsibility for accidents, parents, etc.) remain exempt from punishment. This applies to a particular extent also to Utilitarianism. Popper's proposition to minimize suffering follows the principles of practical philosophy and political practice which could not function according to other maxims. CU with its hedonistic calculation of disregarding pain in favour of a higher quantity of happiness violates these basic rules.

2.3 Irrespective of the fact that NU was originally designed for public policy it can also be applied as moral standard in the meaning of Addendum I to volume II (such as e.g. the Golden Rule) for the personal behaviour of human beings with regard to fellow human beings – containing the ban to inflict pain.

2.4. Thanks to its prohibition to inflict pain NU is also a suitable instrument for dealing with conflicting interests in human relationships and thus acquires a competence of dispute settlement, totally absent in the positively formulated CU which only contains an obligation to act for an end of happiness. It prevents above all actions inflicting pain on others or, expressed in more general terms, actions causing damage to others. In a secondary instance NU provides for helping others whether or not a kind of suffering already exists or is imminent.

2.5. NU thus offers a theory in every way superior to CU both in the field of social pragmatism and as a standard of moral correctness of behaviour between human beings.

3. Popper himself used the term „negative utilitarianism" neither in the core piece of "The Open Society and its Enemies" nor in Addendum I. The adjective "negative" coined by R.N. Smart in his criticism in "Mind" in 1958 was later on randomly used by all critics in order to

establish an opposite version to the classical utilitarianism considered positive. In his reply to the critique of his proposal Popper opines in Addendum I that his "minimum misery principle" as part of the Agenda of Public Policy should be considered as an improvement of some of the ideas of utilitarianism and not as its unique criterion.

Popper's demand for the elimination of suffering rather than the promotion of happiness, the principle the classical utilitarianism is based on, falls within the politics of public authorities as does the latter. The inherent asymmetry in both moral respect and actual practice that the principle of "minimizing suffering" implicitly includes, in addition to the commandment – of an even preceding order – of caring for those suffering, the prohibition to harm others was brought to the attention of Popper by the author in an essay basically dealing with all aspects as referred to in this paper. In his letter dated 21st July, 1984, Popper qualified this essay as excellent and embarked on a lifelong friendship with the author.

When coining the term "negative" utilitarianism for Popper's proposal for an improvement R.N. Smart connected it with Popper's appeal to formulate general moral demands negatively and he understood the minimization of suffering to be the opposite of the maximization of happiness according to classical utilitarianism. This, however, does not apply to the utilitarianism as conceived by Popper and also understood by Smart as social pragmatism of the state and other public authorities. The very appeal to care for those suffering represents a (positive) commandment and requires action. But the general – implicitly included – prohibition to cause suffering unto others as a rule of morals for mutual behaviour among individuals, corresponds exactly to Popper's suggestion to add to clarity in the field of ethics if we formulate demands negatively. It can therefore justly be referred to as a "negative" principle. There should, consequently, be no objection to the further use of the accustomed term "negative utilitarianism" pars pro toto, the more so in order to distinguish Popper's "improved utilitarianism" from other attempts towards a further development (from act-utilitarianism to rule-utilitarianism and descriptive- utilitarianism).

Popper's improved utilitarianism does not contradict the classical utilitarianism. It does not differ from the positive aims of the classical utilitarianism by conflicting negative aims. The overall envisaged target is the same for both: the welfare of the human being. It is only that Popper's utilitarianism is confined to a realistic aim compared with the utopian, never attainable goal of a promised continuous increase of happiness. Popper convincingly demonstrated that such utopias, ever and again politically misused, meet with immediate disaster in his treatises "The Open Society and Its Enemies" and "The Poverty of Historicism" and dedicated the second book (1957): TO THE MEMORY OF THE COUNTLESS MEN, WOMEN AND CHILDREN OF ALL CREEDS AND NATIONS OR RACES WHO FELL VICTIMS TO THE FASCIST AND COMMUNIST BELIEF IN INEXORABLE LAWS OF HISTORICAL DESTINY. Popper's warning, confirmed by historical events, should not go unheeded. His improved utilitarianism transforms the concept of a dangerous utopia into practicable reality in the never ending task of solving human problems.

Bibliography

KARL R. POPPER: The Open Society and Its Enemies, Princeton University Press, Princeton 1966
Die offene Gesellschaft und ihre Feinde, J.C.B. Mohr, Tübingen, Siebente Auflage 1992, Achte Auflage 2003
R. N. SMART: Mind 1958 Vol. 67
J. J. C. SMART: An Outline of a System of Utilitarian Ethics, Melbourne 1961
H.B. ACTON: Aristotelian Society 1963 Suppl. Vol. 37
J.W.N. WATKINS: Aristotelian Society 1963 Suppl. Vol. 37
A.D.M. WALKER: Mind 1974 Vol. 83
K.E. TRANÖY: Asymmetries in Ethics, Inquiry 1967
I. JARVIE und S. PRALONG (editors): Popper's Open Society after 50 Years, Routledge London and New York 1999
J. SHEARMUR: The Political Thought of Karl Popper,
E.KADLEC Praktische Philosophie- heute. Mit K. Popper zur Grundlegung einer Universalmoral, Duncker & Humblot, Berlin 2007

Note

1 Included in the 1992 German edition („ Tatsachen, Maßstäbe und Wahrheit, eine weitere Kritik des Relativismus") revised by Popper himself.

Popper's path from Evolutionary Biology to his late Evolutionary Thinking

Peter Markl

1. Introduction

When Karl Popper evoked his earliest childhood memories it was the face of Charles Darwin which came to his mind since it had left a lasting impression on him, probably before he could even read. The library of his father not only contained most of Darwin's books, but a photograph of Darwin was hung in Simon Popper's study, along with a portrait of Schopenhauer. It was the well-known photograph of the old Darwin, taken in 1881, a year before his death: a long white beard, the face framed by impressive white hair, dark eyes under a big black hat; ready to leave for a rainy walk near Down House he is wrapped in a strange dark raincoat without sleeves, sitting "friendly and very quiet, but a little sad, and a little lonely"[1-4].

Simon Popper studied law at Vienna University and became a close friend and legal partner of Karl Grüb, who was the last liberal Burgomaster of Vienna. After his death in 1898 Simon Popper took over his law firm and moved to a huge department with adjoining office space in the first floor of a house which is today Bauernmarkt Nr. 1. It is the very center of Vienna: looking down the Jasomirgott Straße for a few hundred meters opens the view to the main front of St. Stephan's Cathedral.

Simon Popper, who worked as barrister and solicitor, was a progressive liberal intellectual, a prominent member of a stratum of society which was the main fertile soil for Vienna's cultural achievements in the first third of the 20th century – in music, architecture, painting, literature, philosophy and science. While large parts of the political life were dominated by conservative and clerical institutions, many of the leading scientists propagated liberal ideas. Liberal circles among scientists had already elected Darwin as a corresponding member in 1871 and in 1875 as Honorary member of the Academy of Sciences in Vienna. Darwin's ideas were widely discussed and largely accepted by leading scientists even if they disagreed on a large number of other points. Physics was dominated by the towering figures of Ludwig Boltzmann and Ernst Mach and both were Darwinists of some sort. It was Boltzmann who not only enthusiastically defended atomism and realism, but giving a lecture an thermodynamics in 1886, he already confessed, that he would not hesitate to call the 19th century "Darwin's century". Later he became an "absolute" Darwinist, inventing evolutionary explanations even for subjects where all others would hesitate[5]. (It was inconsequential that Ernst Mach joined Boltzmann in defending elements of an evolutionary epistemology since in his influential book "The analysis of sensations" he had proposed an idealistic ideas in the tradition of Bishop Berkeley, while Darwin's evolutionary biology is a strong corroboration of realism.)

Nevertheless, an echo of Mach's ideas probably reached the very young Karl Popper by discussions with his friend Arthur Arndt, who was some twenty years older than Popper and perhaps even more interested in the Monist movement than Popper's father was. This movement had been founded by pupils of Ernst Mach and Wilhelm Ostwald in 1913 was devoted to the discussion of philosophical aspects of science and scientific philosophy. Arndt invited the 12 year old Karl to join the Monists on their regular Sunday excursions in the Vienna woods and it was probably there that he listened to arguments on Marxism and Darwinism for the first time.

The breakdown of the Austrian empire brought political turmoil, inflation, extreme poverty and hunger to Vienna where the desperate situation culminated in hunger riots in winter 1918/19. Popper was impressed by the social attitude and pacifism of the social democrats (at the time called "socialists") and became a member of the association of socialist pupils of secondary schools ("sozialistische Mittelschüler), participating in their discussion meetings as well as in meetings of socialist university students. He was exposed to Marxist ideas which impressed him to the point of regarding himself as a communist for some month. But a few month later he had an experience which he later regarded as one of the turning points in his life: he experienced deadly violence from close range. On June 15th 1919 he had joined an unarmed demonstration which had gathered in the Hörlgasse – a few hundred meters from the main University building – to help some communists which were under arrest in the central police station. The police opened fire on the crowd killing 20 people and seriously wounding 70 others. Popper was not only shocked by the brutality of the police but he also accused himself of having uncritically accepted the justification Marxists offered for imposing deadly risks on others. They regarded themselves as in possession of a "scientific" law of the development of history which allows them to predict that history will – through a period of class struggle – finally lead to socialism: Intensifying the class struggle would accelerate the coming of socialism which will end the reign of capitalism which would inevitably produce more victims than then the comparatively few victims caused by the socialist revolution.

It was in this emotional context that Popper faced the question if there can be general laws of history for the first time. In which sense can such "laws" – if they exist – be called "scientific"? What was the difference in character between the three theories which had fascinated him lately: the Marxist theory of the development of history, psychoanalytic theories and Einstein's special relativity? Sigmund Freud was a family friend and Popper had done some unpaid work in Alfred Adler's child guidance clinics. He had been introduced to special relativity theory by his friend Max Elstein and was deeply impressed, when on May 29th 1919 relativity theory was gloriously corroborated by a team of the English Royal Astronomical Society which succeeded in measuring the deviation of light under the influence of the gravity field of the sun – an effect which had been predicted by Einstein in 1916.

The problem of the existence and status of historical "laws" had previously been discussed intensively in the context of various philosophies of history and there had also been prominent previous attempts to propose such laws modelled in analogy to Darwin's evolutionary theory . But Popper did not mention biological evolutionary theory in one of his publications before 1930. No doubt attempts to support vague talk on "laws of history" – for instance by the philosopher Herbert Spencer, who's evolutionary philosophy was based on wildly speculative extrapolations from Darwin's ideas on the evolution of life on earth – formed part of the problem horizon in the background of Popper's thinking when he started to work on the two volumes of "Die beiden Grundprobleme der Erkenntnistheorie" ("The Two Fundamental Problems in the Theory of Knowledge"): originally 1200 pages, written by Popper in the time left from teaching at the Pedagogic Institute of City of Vienna[6].

The manuscript of these volumes had disappeared after it had been deposited with friends when Popper hastily prepared his emigration to New Zealand in 1937. (In his contribution to the preset volume Troels Eggers Hansen tells the unbelievable story of the search for this text in the 1970´s and how he finally edited a book based on the parts which could still be found).

It is in this book that book Popper had already referred to Herbert Spencer Jennings book on the „Behavior of the Lower Organism" (1906) where Jennings sees the movements of unicellular organism as exploratory movements in a "search" for better living conditions. Popper uses this interpretation of these exploratory movements to introduce the central conjectures of his epistemology: from the criticism of induction to his comprehensive theory of the growth of knowledge actively created by conjectures (hypothesis, anticipations) and refutations: „ "Nicht durch Abstraktion oder Verallgemeinerung aus den Sinneswahrnehmungen kommen wir nach deduktivistischer Auffassung zu unserem Erfahrungswissen, sondern durch Ausprobieren von Anticipationen, die dem "Material" der Rezeption vorläufig zugeordnet werden. Ob diese vorläufige Zuordnung wieder aufgegeben wird oder nicht, darüber entscheidet ihr biologischer Wert. Die Methode der Entscheidung ist eine selektive: Erweisen sich die Antizipationen als wertlos, so werden sie ausgemerzt; sie werden entweder durch andere Reaktionen ersetzt oder ihr "Träger", der regierende Organismus, geht mit ihnen zugrunde. Die Bewährung an der Umwelt entscheidet über das Schicksal der präformierten Anticipationen. Es ist die Methode von Versuch und Irrtum, die Methode der Selektion".

Unfortunately the publisher found Poppers manuscript to long by far and insisted on cutting it down to 240 pages in print. This was mercilessly executed by Popper and his uncle Walter Schiff. The result was published in 1934 as "Logik der Forschung"[7]. The dramatic shortening of the manuscript could not be achieved without sacrifices and it is unfortunate that the explicit references on evolutionary theory were among the victims. All that is left in the "Logik der Forschung" is a remark made in the context of a discussion on the selection of theories where it is stated that one should expose "das zu überprüfende System in jeder Weise einer Falsifikation"; "aber "nicht die Rettung unhaltbarer Systeme ist ihr Ziel, sondern: in möglichst strengem Wettbewerb das relativ haltbarste auszuwählen".

But when Popper translated „Logik der Forschung" for he first English edition, he returned to strongly emphasizing the biological analogy by inserting: "According to my proposal, what characterizes the empirical method is its manner of exposing to falsification, in every conceivable way, the system to be tested. Its aim is not to safe untenable systems, but, on the contrary, to select the one which is by comparison the fittest, by exposing them all to the fiercest struggle for survival"[8].

In spite of being aware of its limits Popper never abandoned the analogy between the processes driving biological evolution and the growth of human knowledge. The paragraphs contained in his earliest book were the seed for the evolutionary epistemology which he developed in the last decades of his life. In 1974 – more than 50 years after working on "Die beiden Grundprobleme der Erkenntnistheorie" – Popper went even further and wrote in a reply to Donald T. Campbell's essay on Popper's evolutionary epistemology: "The main task of the theory of human knowledge is to understand it as continuous with animal knowledge; and to understand also its discontinuity – if any – from animal knowledge". The late Popper never became tired in emphasizing his view that there is a unity in actively promoting the growth of knowledge – "from the amoeba to Einstein", biological evolution being just one stage in the unfolding creativity of life[9].

Popper's work in the years after 1933 stood increasingly in the shadow of the threatening political development which led from the closing of the Austrian society by the suspension of parliamentary democracy by an authoritative Christian-Social regime into civil war and finally – after Popper's emigration in 1937 – to the military annexation by Hitler's troops and the end of Austria in 1938 leaving the country under the dictatorship of Austrian and German National Socialists.

Nowadays one can hardly imagine the stress of Popper's life in the years from 1932 to 1937:

He was a "Hauptschullehrer" lacking academic credentials, with a leftist past and no illusions with regard to an academic future in Austria. In 1932 his father and a sister had died and it was left to him to support his mother. In his admirable biography Malachi Haim Hacohen[10] has described the depressing political and economic circumstances which were a heavy burden for Karl and Henny Popper in these years. In spite of all this Popper had – by a seemingly endless capacity for intense work – achieved international recognition for papers not only in epistemology and methodology of science, but also in probability theory, logic and even quantum mechanics. (Popper regarded it as "the greatest compliment he ever received " when Niels Bohr and Albert Einstein came to a lecture he gave in Princeton in 1950 and stayed to discuss with him indeterminism in physics long after all others had left the auditorium. Popper was proud of his friends among scientists and emphasized that he had known them, before some of them – like John Eccles, Peter Medawar, Hermann Bondi – became Nobelists).

It is only a fair judgment if Malachi Haim Hacohen states that the epistemological revolution initiated with "Die beiden Grundprobleme" are "a high point in twenties century philosophy". The emphases shifted from personal subjective knowledge to objective scientific knowledge obtained by hypothetical conjectures followed by their critical discussion and empirical tests to eliminate errors. The same holds for the methodology of science proposed in "Logik der Forschung". Sir Peter Medawar regarded Popper as "incomparably the greatest philosopher of science ever" and many scientist – especially among the bioscientists – agree.

In 1935, however, the fact that Popper had gained international reputation in different fields, did not help to improve his precarious situation in Vienna. In his Autobiography he wrote: "I expected, from 1929 on, the rise of Hitler; I expected the annexation, of Austria by Hitler, in some form or other; and I expected the war against the west". Partly in order to improve his job prospects by documenting his competence in methodology of sociology he began drafting a paper which consisted in an outline of the ideas he had developed on the "laws of history" since the problem was posed to him when he analyzed the reaction of his Marxist friends on the bloody incidence in the Hörlgasse in 1919.

For Popper the intellectual problem situation had dramatically changed: he now saw it against the background of the methodology of science he had developed in writing "Die beiden Grundprobleme" and the "Logik der Forschung". The lecture he drafted in 1935 already contained the most important ideas which were – after being intensively reorganized, revised and elaborated in Popper's first years in New Zealand – published in 1944 and 1945 as three papers in "Economia". It took another decade till they finally became available in book form. After Italian (1954) and French (1955) editions the first English book edition was published in 1957[11]. Popper had shown that vague analogies between the theory of biological evolution and theories describing the "evolution" of societies can not be used to support historicist evolutionary "laws" because they are based in misunderstandings not only of biological evolutionary theory but of science in general.

It was in this context of social methodology and political philosophy that Popper returned to the discussion of the theory of biological evolution. And in some sense it was a lucky point in time to resume writing on evolutionary theory since in autumn 1935 he was invited to give a series of lectures in England where he stayed from September 1935 to mid June 1936, interrupted only by a Christmas visit to Vienna. On his return trip to London in January 1936 he spend a few days in Brussels where he gave an informal lecture on his ideas before offering them in a more formal presentation in Hayek's seminar at the London School of Economics.

His stay in England was an uplifting experience: he later called his visit "a breath of fresh air". He was "kindly received" by Alfred J Ayer who – at the time a young English philosopher who had participated as a guest in some "Vienna Circle" sessions – looked him after "as a hen looks after a chick". He made personal acquaintance with some of the leading English philosopher, and he met others who later became close personal friends: Hayek, Gombrich and Schrödinger.

And he met J. H. Woodger, a biologist with a strong interest in philosophy of biology, who invited him for a couple of days to what Popper later describes as a "meeting at the old windmill at Hunstanton, in some of the most pleasant surroundings". It was in this meeting that he met – among others – J. D. Bernal, J. B. S. Haldane, Dorothy Hodgkin, and C. H. Waddington. J. B. S. Haldane and J. D. Bernal – at the time both members of the communist party – were in the midst of their thirties and at the peak of their scientific creativity. Haldane had published a series of papers which he summarized in 1932 in his book "The Causes of Evolution": 60 pages, a classic, which is still in print, written to refute the intense criticism of Darwinian selection theory between 1900 – 1930. Haldane – and others like R. A. Fisher and S. Wright – had shown that selection theory is compatible with Mendelian genetics. This was an essential step on the way to what is now often referred to as the "modern synthesis" in evolutionary theory. This "syntheses" was achieve in the years from 1937 – 1952 by some of the leading evolutionary theorists who wrote books to document that their special field which had until then developed in a certain independence from the development in neighboring fields, increasingly became mosaic stones fitting in a much larger unified picture. The major architects of this much more comprehensive view of the forces that formed the history of life on earth were the geneticist Theodosius Dobzhansky (Genetics and the Origin of Species, 1937), the zoologist Ernst Mayr (Systematics and the Origin of species, 1942), the botanist G. Ledyard Stebbins (Variation and Evolution in Plants, 1950) and the paleontologist George Gaylord Simpson (The Major Features of Evolution, 1953).

2. Return to evolutionary biology in the midst of efforts to establish philosophy of biology as a new field

Since the days at "the old windmill at Hunstanton" Popper was always fortunate in having made personal acquaintance with leading evolutionary biologists. After his return to England he was interested to renew and enlarge his contacts with leading scientists. He now "formally" joined the Theoretical Biology Club in 1946 where he first met Peter Medawar who became a close personal friend and wrote in his memoirs that "Popper most earnestly tried to draw out the findings and opinions of his scientific colleagues and this made his presence invaluable"[12].

Since then Popper had been one of the rare philosophers who caught the attention of British biologists. In the fiftieth and sixties the biological community everywhere became deeply divided in a struggle between "organismic" biologists and a new generation of biochemists, molecular biologists and molecular geneticists whom many saw as unwelcome newcomers in the competition for research funding and academic positions. Some of the most prominent initiators of these fields had come from physics and imported into biology a methodological rigor that had been unknown in some more traditionally oriented biological fields or difficult to apply in the analysis of complex biological systems.

The great biologist Ernst Mayr, a friend of Karl Popper, was not only one of the fathers of the "modern synthetic evolutionary theory", but also a fascinating and polemic historian of science who can hardly be surpassed in his scepticism directed against a methodology imported from physical sciences. He rather angrily stated that in the fiftieths and sixtieth Popper was very much "in fashion" and every biologist he knew claimed to be a "Popperian"[13]. (Like many polemicists, Mayr was not a good listener or reader: He cites Popper quite often but misinterprets him almost every time.)

In the early seventies some "organismic" evolutionary theorists felt that one of their problems was the continuing dominance of a general scientific methodology which originated in physics and prevented the recognition of the "autonomy of biology". They persuaded the Rockefeller foundation to host a conference to discuss the dominance of the methodology of physics in the emerging field of philosophy of biology: Can one really hope to reduce biology to chemistry and chemistry to physics ? The conference was held in Villa Serbelloni in Bellagio from 9 – 16 September 1972. It was there that Popper met Francisco Ayala, Theodosius Dobzhansky, John Eccles (Nobel Prize 1963), Gerald Edelman (Nobel Prize 1972), Peter Medawar (Nobel Prize 1960) , Ledyard Stebbins and Jacques Monod (Nobel Prize 1965). (Monod was an admirer of Popper, had written a preface to the French edition of the Logik der Forschung and persuaded his son Philippe Monod to translate the first volume of the "Open Society"). Popper contributed an important paper on "Scientific Reduction and the Essential Incompleteness of All Science"[14]

Now, with 36 years distance and in the light of a tremendous increase in biological knowledge, one is tempted to conclude that the center of many of the discussions in the seventies and eighties was not so much the autonomy of biology or a methodology illegitimately imported from physics but problems in the application of Poppers methodology to hierarchical levels of increasing complexity – levels as they emerged from the simplest living systems to – for instance – the human brain. Sir Martin Reese has recently promoted awareness to the fact, that physics had overwhelming success in the description of simple systems – the micro world dominated by quantum physics and cosmology dominated by gravitational forces. The main challenge now is in the description of the world in between – complexity is the real frontier[15].

Ernst Mayr, who had become a living witness of the history of evolutionary biology when he died in 2005 at the age of 101, never got tired in criticizing what he saw as the inadequacy of Poppers methodology and to illustrate the difficulties of its application in biology. Even when he acknowledges that an author clearly proceeded in a "Popperian" method of conjectures and refutations – as Darwin did for his evolutionary theory – Mayr offers a different account. In his admirable (and often rather biased) treatise on the history of biological thought[16] he describes the logic of Darwin's theory of natural selection as starting from five observations leading to three (inductive) interferences:

Mayr wrote:

"Population ecology teaches:

Fact 1 All species have such great potential fertility that their population size would increase exponentially if all newborn individuals would again reproduce successfully.
Fact 2 Except for minor annual fluctuations and occasional major fluctuations populations normally display stability.
Fact 3 Natural resources are limited. In a stable environment they remain relatively constant.

Inference 1 There must be a fierce struggle for existence among individuals of a population, resulting in the survival of only part of the progeny of each generation.

Genetics teaches:

Fact 4 Every population displays a large variation among it's individuals.
Fact 5 Much of this variation is heritable.

Inference 2   Survival in the struggle for existence is not random but depends in part on the hereditary constitution of the surviving individuals.
Inference 3   Over the generation this process of natural selection will lead to a continuing gradual change of populations, that is, to evolution and to the production of new species.

In analyzing Darwin's great book historians of ideas have shown that he was keen to demonstrate that his theory was conceived in accordance with the best methodology available[17] He even opened the book with quotations from Francis Bacon (1561 – 1626) and the contemporary Baconian William Whewell (1794 – 1866). And he wrote in his Autobiography: "In worked on true Baconian principles, and without any theory collected acts on a wholesale scale"[18]. This, however, is – as Popper liked to illustrate by telling an anecdote from his Viennese years – simply impossible: if someone is asked to "observe" he will inevitably have to ask: Observe ? What ?

Darwin – of course – knew that. In a letter he noted: "How odd it is that anyone should not see that all observation must be for or against some view ... if it is to be of any service"[19]

And he presented the main theses of his great book[20] in the famous "long argument", which consists of a concatenation of hypotheses followed by a critical evaluation of their corroboration – not unlike an abstract of a modern paper:

If, during the long course of ages and under varying conditions of life, organic bearings vary at all in their several parts of their organization, and I thing this cannot be disputed; if there be, owing to the high geometrical powers of increase of each species, at some age, season or year, a severe struggle for life, and this certainty cannot be disputes; then, considering the infinite complexity in relations of all organic beings to each other, to their conditions of existence, causing an infinite diversity in structure, constitution, and habits, to be advantageous to them, I thing it would be the most extraordinary fact that no variation ever had occurred useful to each being's own welfare, in the same way as so many variations have occurred useful to man. But if variations useful to any organic being do occur, assuredly individuals thus characterized will have the best chance to being preserved in the struggle for life; and from the strong principle of inheritance they will tend to prudence offspring similarly characterized.

This principle of preservation, I have called, for the sake of brevity, Natural selection".

And he added:

"This preservation of favorable variations and the rejection of injurious variations I call Natural Selection. Variations neither useful or injurious would not be affected by natural selection, and would be left a fluctuating element"[21].

One can even demonstrate that in his methodological practice Darwin was an exemplary precursor of Popper. Throughout his book he followed the advice to state in advance when he would regard his conjecture as falsified:

"If it could be demonstrated that any complex organ existed, which could not possibly have been formed by numerous, successive, slight modifications, my theory would absolutely break down" [22].

"Natural selection cannot possibly produce any modification in any one species exclusively for the good of another species. If it could be proved that any part of the structure of one species had been formed for the exclusive good of another species, it would annihilate my theory, for such could not have been produced through natural selection"[23].

"If numerous species, belonging to the same genera or families, have really started into life all at once, that fact would be fatal to the theory of descent with slow modification through natural selection"[24].

Darwin devoted a whole chapter of his book to the discussion of what he regarded as "*by far the most serious difficulty*" for his theory: the explanation of the evolution of complex social structure of insect societies by Natural selection – as we now know a problem which was definitely out of reach given the theories of genetics available in Darwin's days. This is discussed in a chapter on "Instinct"[25]. He opens the chapter in a very "Popperian" way by refusing to attempt any definition of the – now extinct – term "instinct – because every one "*understands what is meant*" in this specific context. But in evaluating his hypothesis by comparing it to observations he remained critical and concluded:

"I do not pretend that the facts given in this chapter strengthen in any degree my theory; but none of the cases of difficulty, to the best of my judgment, annihilate it".

Darwin did not only invite refutations by explicitly pointing to crucial arguments in his theory. He had always been his own "spin doctor": in the years from 1821 to his death he wrote and received about 15.000 letters which were one of the sources for the six revised editions of the "Origin of Species" – a book which was a sort of "Work in Progress": in 1859 the first edition contained about 4000 sentences but Darwin had rewritten about 3000 of them for the sixth edition in 1872[26] It is very important to make a clear distinction between different parts of Darwin's evolutionary theory because they had a very different fate: Darwin's historical conjectures on the common origin of all living organism and their evolution which forms the history of life had almost universally been accepted in the 1860´s by most of the knowledgeable experts. The problem situation was, however, quite different for Darwin's theory on the mechanism which caused evolutionary change – especially the theory of natural selection. Of course this theory met ideologically motivated criticism but for Darwin this was not what bothered him most. It was the scientific criticism contained in a review by Fleeming Jenkin published in a copy of the "North British" review which landed in Darwin's desk in 1867. Darwin later wrote

"Fleeming Jenkin has given me much trouble, but has been of more real use to me than other essays or reviews"[27].

It was a model of interdisciplinary criticism: Jenkin was professor of electric engineering at the university of Glasgow, a student of William Thompson, who later became Lord Kelvin. Jenkin pointed out that in 1866 William Thompson – with all the authority of a "hard" science like physics – had attempted to derive an estimation of the age of the earth based on its cooling rate. He arrived on an age that was much to small to allow a succession of all the small steps Darwin needed for his "descent by modification in small steps". (We now know that this estimate was wrong – mainly because Lord Kelvin could not take into account an energy source which was unknown at the time: the energy produced by the decay of radioactive element in the inner of the earth).

But Jenkins had an even more deadly second argument directed against Darwin's "Pangenesis" theory of the genetic transmission of heritable characteristics from generation to generation. According to this theory the genetic material of parents is mixed in the next generation very much in analogy to the mixing of two liquids. If either mother or father would be lucky in possessing "good" genetic material mixing in the next generation would result in a dilution which increases from generation to generation. Only if both parents would be "favorable variations" this favors could be "preserved" in the next generation but mixing in the following generation would make it increasingly improbable that this would – by chance – happen again. Unless – of course – that a great number of newly generated "positive variations" could compensate for the increasing dilution.

Many of the revisions in Darwin's revised editions of "The Origins" are attempts to come to terms with this type of genetic arguments, but it is clear that – given the state of knowledge of genetic mechanism at the time – it was a hopeless battle. Darwin did not know the papers of Gregor Mendel and even after their rediscovery in 1900 their implications were hardly understood for some time and frequently misinterpreted as advocating rare and large mutations. When G. B. S. Haldane wrote his "The causes of evolution" in 1932 he discussed the criticism directed against Darwin's selection theory in the years from 1900 – 1930 and headed the first chapter with the quote *"Darwin is dead"* and before summarizing the state of the discussion by stating: *"The criticism of Darwinism has been so thorough going that a few biologists and many laymen regarded it as more or less exploded".*

This had already become history when four years later Haldane met Popper at the windmill but – from a vaguely Popperian methodological point of view – some problems in testing selection theory remained in spite of the breathtaking advances of evolutionary theory.

3. Problems in testing selection theory by too naive ideas

Now – almost eighty years after the days at the windmill – we have a molecular theory of the generation of genetic variation, we know molecular mechanism for the transmission of genetic information between generations and we know that in addition the natural selection there is a number of other mechanism which influence evolutionary change.

(Today there still is a large literature on difficulties in testing selection theory, for instance by Richard Lewontin[28] or Massimo Pigliucci and Jonathan Kaplan[29].)

It might, however, be useful to illustrate the problems involved in testing the applications of modern population genetics by a too simple minded Popperian falsificationist methodology before continuing by a discussion of Poppers problems with evolutionary theory and the "addition" he proposed as a solution – his version of an active Darwinism.

Richard Lewontin, one of the leading population geneticists and evolutionary theorists, has occasionally characterized himself as a "dialectical" biologist probably because of his strong interest in ideas which go beyond the main stream of evolutionary thinking. (The problems he discussed in this context have many resemblances to views Karl Popper discusses in his later publications.)

Lewontin gave a brilliant illustration for the difficulties faced by philosophers attempting to transfer epistemological and methodological insights gained by analyzing the most advanced physics – relativity theory and quantum mechanics – to the analysis of the new evolutionary and population genetics. With the new physics of the first third of the 20 century the main challenge was to explain the apparent contradictions between the mathematical structure of these theories and their physical interpretations with the experience of the every day world of mesoscopic dimensions. Does physics really describe reality or just what we can find out about reality by theory and experiment ? In which sense do all this particles and matter waves exist ?

Lewontin[28] wrote: *"The source of philosophical interest in evolutionary genetics had not been, as in physics, the fundamentally paradoxical ontological properties of the objects of inquiry. Organism seem to behave in quite commonsensical ways, and their history does not pose problem that seem to confound rationality. The philosophical issues arise not out of a lack of intuitively reasonable explanations of what we observe, but on the contrary, from a superfluidity of such explanations. The problem is how to decide in any particular case which of the reasonable explanations to believe. It is the epistemologist's paradise".*

In population genetics the problem situation is quite different from the typical situation in physics. Evolution is an irreducibly historical process: *"On the one hand the process is a consequence of a large set of universal basic biological mechanism that are not themselves contingent in the way in which they enter into explanatory causal chains but – on the other hand – the quantitative effects they have on the evolution of an organisms arise from properties of the organism themselves – for example, whether they reproduce sexually – and from autonomous, independently acting external forces like physical environmental factors or the presence of other species:* " The explanation of the present state of organism and the prediction of their future state, must be considered in terms of universal mechanism whose operation is historically contingent, both because of the importance of initial conditions and because of autonomous externalities that have their own history".

The complexity of this problem situation will inevitably frustrate anyone approaching evolutionary problems with expectations formed in analyzing much simpler problems which have dominated physics in the past: *"Like other scientists, population geneticists have been educated to believe in a naïve univocal model of science, a model that takes the discovery of universals to be the final validation of scientific inquiries and accurate quantitative evaluation of all relevant causal variables to be the mark of a truly scientific explanation. They are therefore dissatisfied with a science that says that "x can happen" or that "x sometimes happens" or even "z often happens". Moreover, in the explanation of a specific case they regard it as a defeat to be allowed to say only "x could have been the cause of the observation, y could have been a significant factor, and z certainly played an important causal role".*

Yet for evolutionary phenomena which are influenced by many weakly determining and interacting causal pathways with the result of the interactions depending in historical contingency, this is the best one can achieve even if one has adequate empirical data.

There are, of course, other cases, in which organism are exposed to a large selection pressure which dominates all other evolutionary forces. In such cases it is not too difficult to predict which of the different organism will have relatively better chances to survive to reproductive age and thus contribute to the next generation.

Population geneticists express these chances as fitness values but this is not – as Popper[30] once remarked "- *almost tautological"*. He wrote[31]: "Fitness is defined by modern evolutionists as survival value, and can be measured by actual success in survival: There is hardly any possibility of testing a theory as feeble as this". But this is a misunderstanding caused by the technical definition of fitness in modern population genetics – a misunderstanding Popper initially shared with some highly respected biologists and many critics. The great evolutionary theorist Steven Jay Gould tried to correct this mistake by pointing out that it was Darwin's view that certain traits make an organism a better candidate for survival than competing organism: *"Certain morphological, physiological, and behavioral traits should be superior a priori as design for living in new envi-*

ronments. These traits confer fitness by an engineer's criterion of good design, not by the empirical fact of their survival and spread"[32].

In his later publications Popper has returned to Darwin when he simply emphasized that better adapted individuals have a superior chance to reproduce. In this context Popper pointed out that other terms frequently used in discussing evolutionary theory – terms like "natural selection" or "struggle for survival" – are irreparably metaphoric and can be very misleading[33].

Most biologists are of course aware of the metaphorical character of some of their concepts most of the time – they use these terms as convenient abbreviations – but it can be argued that thinking in these terms sometimes limits the range of ideas they are willing to consider in preliminary discussions of the problem situation. This can again be illustrated by again quoting an eminent population geneticist who has found a polemical formulation for the unnoticed detrimental effects. In 1971 William B. Provine has published a short and lucid history of "The Origins of Theoretical Population Genetics"[34] from Darwin's time to Haldine's "The cause of Evolution" in 1932. When he added an afterword for the new addition in 2001 he wrote some very polemic paragraphs:

"Natural selection is not a mechanism. Natural selection does not act on anything, nor does it select (for or against), force, maximize, create, modify, shape, operate, drive, favor, maintain, push, or adjust. Natural selection does nothing". For Provine the idea that natural selection is a "force" should be classified as in the same kind as "phlogiston" or Newton's "ether" – a relict from history, legitimately and useful in Darwin's time, but inexcusable for evolutionists now. And Provine adds: " Natural selection is the necessary outcome of discernible and often quantifiable causes. Some of these causes produce heritable differences between individuals of most populations and between populations. The possible production of offspring is immense in any species and a "struggle for existence" occurs. A complicated demographic process follows, resulting in organism adapted to their environment, as long as the environments don't change too rapidly. Understanding natural selection as the result of specific causes requires the researchers to understand ecological settings, life histories and development in relation to differential leaving of offspring".

This is of course a kind of a research program which is vigorously investigated today and has already yielded results which – according to some commentators – go beyond the consensus opinion which was in the center of the modern synthetic theory of evolution.

4. Poppers changing views on the scientific status of evolutionary theory

Written seven years after Popper's death, Provine's polemic paragraphs suggest that Popper's previous discussions of evolutionary problems can be seen as contributions to an early phase of this research program. As Brian Magee observed Popper was always *"the odd man out"* in the different scientific discussion groups he joined – respected because of his primary competence in methodology and philosophy but keenly aware of his "amateurism". Ernst Mayr had contacted him in 1973 expressing delight in seeing him interested in the emerging philosophy of biology. But in 1991 when Popper enthusiastically collaborated with Günter Wächtershäuser on the origin of life, he wrote to Mayr: *"I am an extreme layman in this field – the extreme opposition to a specialist. I am, simply, very curious about evolution, and I love to think about it. And I love theories"*[35].

It is, however, not easy to follow the somewhat tortuous path of the development of Poppers ideas on of evolutionary biology and it will not be attempted here. (Interested readers may consult the annotated list of relevant publications in the annex).

While biologists had problems in imagining how to falsify their evolutionary conjectures, Popper had problems with the theory of national selection. In the late thirties, when he worked on "The poverty of Historicism" he found evolutionary philosophies modeled in analogy to biological evolution, hardly interesting. But in 1965 he confessed that his thesis of the continuity of the mechanism for generating the growth of knowledge – from amoeba to Einstein – had become one of the centers of his interest. In 1974 he devoted a whole chapter of his autobiography to selection theory, which he now regarded as "almost tautological", not really a falsifiable scientific theory, but something which can become immensely prolific for science – a heuristically fertile metaphysical research program with situational logic at the core. Certain problem situations are best described as examples of a situational logic: If there is a framework of limited constancy which contains entities of limited variability making them fit for this framework to a different degree resulting in different chances to reproduce, than Darwinian selection will follow with "almost" logical necessity. (Religiously motivated critics of evolutionary theory were very happy with this characterization of selection theory – as not really science – and, judged by the Bibles of the Intelligent Design Movement, some still are).

But then – in 1977 – Popper again changed his mind on the scientific status of selection theory. He continued to emphasized that selection theory functions as heuristic program. But he was again willing to regard it as a scientific theory albeit only weakly testable.

He explained this change of view with arguments which were rather confusing for many readers. Following his methodological advise that one should always criticize a theory in its strongest possible form, he assumed that all functional complex organs or behavior are products of natural selection. He then reminded his readers that Darwin had already seen sexual selection as another mechanism driving evolution. Seen from this point of view he concluded that natural selection was not only a falsifiable scientific theory, but a theory which has already been falsified.

The years from the early seventies to Poppers death in 1994 saw the establishment of philosophy of biology as a special discipline of philosophy of science – just as the great architects of the modern syntheses of evolutionary biology had hoped when they began their dialog with Popper. For the next generation of scientists and philosophers Popper was already a celebrity, inspiring in his methodology but remote from their everyday scientific problems. Some of them contacted him because Poppers methodology had encouraged them in their work just as it had encouraged John Eccles since their days in New Zealand . The Australian immunologist Edward Steel had written a book on "Somatic Selection and Adaptive Evolution: On the Inheritance of Acquired characteristics" and cited Popper as one of his methodological inspirations to embark on such a risky venture[36] . Steel contacted Popper and found him extremely interested in some type of rehabilitation of Lamarckismus but – according to the consensus opinion of the experts – Steel failed. Initially Popper had been quite enthusiastic and Popper's support definitely helped to draw the attention of specialists like Peter Medawar to Steel's work[37].

In his attempt to improve evolutionary theory Popper was predominantly interested in papers which promised important theoretical advances. He had an extensive correspondence and extensively used telephone calls to discuss his problems with trusted experts.

Günter Wächtershäuser is an example of another scientist who – initially – got the attention of the experts mainly because of Popper's support. However, Wächtershäuser is a very different case. He has written some papers in which he extensively discussed how Poppers methodology guided him to find an approach to his great problem – the earliest chemical stages of the Origin of life .

In spite of fierce opposition Wächtershäuser made his point very efficiently. According to his theory life might have started in an Iron-Sulfur World and have a chemo-autographic origin: the very first steps being purely chemical consisting in chemical reactions on the two dimensional surface of pyrite which can supply the necessary energy. This is an alternative to the conjectures that life somehow originated in a "primordial "soup". Wächtershäuser has elaborated his ideas in considerable detail[38]. They are still subject of controversial discussions[39, 40], but they have already reached some standard textbooks[41].

Wächtershäuser, who had met Popper in 1982 at the European Forum in Alpbach, became one of Popper's close friends. In the biographical memoirs of the Royal Society – which had elected Popper as a member in 1976 – David Miller wrote, that for years they spent many hours weekly on the telephone discussing every aspect of the theory with tremendous enthusiasm[42].

In conversation with the next generation of philosophers one can frequently hear how much they were impressed by Popper; and Popper was – of course – one of the most prominent philosophers discussed in the first generation of the books on philosophy of biology which were being written. It is, however, hard to find written documents that can serve as a hint that Popper had much interest in their philosophical papers.

The situation is, however, different for the next generation of evolutionary theorists. In spite of Popper's intense interest in basic questions of evolutionary theory there are only occasional remarks scattered in Popper's papers and they are too sketchy to be cited as essential contributions to the discussion of problem situations which had increasingly shifted away from Popper's point of view. It is remarkable that this trend has turned in the last twenty years. "Active Darwinism" in its various forms – which had since long been an essential component of Popper's epistemology – is in the center of interest among evolutionary biologists.

5. Active Darwinism

In his last years Popper's main interest in evolutionary theory was focused on attempts to demonstrate the limit of the broad consensus achieved in the forties and fifties under the frame of the "modern synthetic theory". He wanted to point to problems he regarded as open problems which were neglected by the scientific establishment – his friend Peter Medawar included. (Popper was not always fortunate in the selection of the arguments he attacked and sometimes in his criticism seen in rather dubious company. Medawar – for instance – had pointed out that he regarded some of Poppers ideas on the genetic basis of behavior as beyond repair). Poppers wanted to find a theory which could be regarded as an alternative theory to natural selection – as a first step to go beyond the synthetic theory.

After Popper's death in 1994 bioscientists developed a great number of new experimental techniques which have been applied in a large variety of fields and generated a stream of fascinating results – for instance in molecular developmental genetics, developmental biology, neurophysiology, behavioural genetics and others. These results have already changed the problem situation in old fields and brought old question within experimental reach. Today an increasing number of evolutionary biologists see their field as already being beyond the "modern" synthetic theory – progressing to a much more comprehensive evolutionary theory which Eva Jablonka and Marion J. Lamb[43, 44] describe in their fascinating and easily readable book "Evolution in four Dimensions : Genetic, Epigenetic, Behavioral, and Symbolic Variation in the History of Life". There is an increasing number of books and articles which arrive at a similar conclusions – for instance by Mary Jane Eberhard[45, 46], Eytan Avital and Eva Jablonka[47], Bruce Weber and D. J. Depew[48], Peter Richerson and Robert Boyd[49] and John Odling-Smee[50].

They summarize the present state of knowledge on subjects like the role of niche construction in evolution or the different versions of the "Baldwin" effect – subjects which Popper shortly discussed in his plea for an "active" Darwinism. In contrast to the opinion of many main stream biologists three decades ago active Darwinism is not a bombastic term for a triviality or misleading or simply false or maybe existent but rare and unimportant. It is an important component of the creativity of life. For Popper this includes human creativity which is always in danger by restrictions on human freedom.

Notes and references

1 Karl Popper: Unending Quest. An Intellectual Autobiography. Routledge Classics. 1992; originally published in 1974 as part of [2].

2. The Philosophy of Karl Popper, edited by Paul Schilpp as Volume 14/1 and 14/2 in the Series "Library of Living Philosophers", Open Court Pubblishing Co., Illinois, 1974.
3. Karl Popper: "Natural Selection and the Emergence of Mind". Chapter 6 in [4]
4. Evolutionary Epistemology. Theory of Rationality and Knowledge. Edited by Gerard Radnitzky and W. W. Bartley, III., Open Court La Salle, 1997.
5. Engelbert Broda: Wissenschaft, Verantwortung, Frieden. Franz Deuticke, Wien, 1985. Seite 47.
6. Karl Popper: Die beiden Grundprobleme der Erkenntnistheorie. Herausgegeben von Troels Eggers Hansen, Mohr Siebeck, Tübingen, 1979.
7. Karl Popper: Logik der Forschung. Julius Springer Verlag, Wien. First edition 1934 printed in 1935.
8. Karl Popper: The Logic of Scientific Discovery. Hutchinson & Co., London, 1959.
9. p. 1061 in Vol. 14/2 of [2].
10. Malachi Haim Hacohen: Karl Popper. The Formative Years 1902 – 1945. Politics and Philosophy in Interwar Vienna. Cambridge University Press. 2000.
11. Karl Popper: The Poverty of Historicism, Routledge & Kegan Paul, London 1957.
12. Peter Medawar: Memoir of a Thinking Radish. An Autobiography. Oxford University Press. 1988; p.85.
13. Ernst Mayr: This is biology. Harvard University Press. 1997.
14. Karl Popper: Scientific Reduction and the Essential Incompleteness of All Science.Chapter 16 in : Studies in the Philosophy of Biology, Edited by F. J. Ayala & T. Dobzhansky. Macmillan 1974.
15. Martin Rees: Explaining the Universe. Chapter 3 in: Explanations. Styles of Explanation in Science. Edited by John Cornwell. Oxford University Press. 2004.
16. Ernst Mayer: The Growth of Biological Thought. Diversity, Evolution, and Inheritance.
Harvard University Press, 1982. p. 479.
17. Tim Lewens: Darwin. Routledge, 2007. Chapter 4, pages 97 – 107.
18. Charles Darwin. Autobiographies. Edited by M. Neve and S. Messenger. Penguin Classics 2004. page 72.
19. More letters of Charles Darwin, edited by Francis Darwin and A. C. Seward, Appleton, New York, 2003. Vol. I, p 195.
20. Charles Darwin: On The Origin of Species by Means of Natural Selection First Edition 1859 by J. Murray, London, 1859. Reprinted by Gramercy Books in 1976.
21. p. 131 in [20].
22. p. 219 in [20].
23. p. 228 in [20].
24. p. 309 in [20].
25. p. 69 in [20].
26. Charles Darwin: Charles Darwin's The Origin of Species: A Variorum Text. Edited by Morse Peckham, University of Pennsylvania Press, 2006.

27 Janet Brown: Darwin. Vol. 2 : The Power of Place. The Origins and after – the years of fame. Pimlico , London. 1995. p. 282.
28 Richard Lewontin: What do Population Geneticists Know and How do they Know it ? Chapter 9 in: Biology and Epistemology. Edited by Richard Creath and Jane Maienschein, Cambridge University Press, 2000.
29 Pigliucci, Massimo, Jonathan Kaplan: Making Sense of Evolution. The Conceptual Foundations of Evolutionary Biology. University of Chicago Press, 2006, Chapter 10: Testing biological hypothesis.
30 Karl Popper: p. 199 of [1].
31 Karl Popper: p. 198 of [1].
32 Steven Jay Gould: Darwin's Untimely Burial. Chapter 3 in Conceptual issues in Evolutionary Biology. An Anthology. Edited by Elliott Sober, 1st Edition 1984.
33 Transcript of the discussion on the lecture Popper held at the Gesellschaft der Ärzte Wien on May 28th 1986. Popper Archive.
34 William B. Provine: The Origins of Theoretical Population Genetics. With a new Afterword. University of Chicago Press 2001, p. 199.
35 Karl Popper to Ernst Mayr, January 1, 1991.b 551,f.4).
36 Edward Steel: Somatic Selection and Adaptive Evolution: On the Inheritance of Acquired characteristics, 2nd edition, University of Chicago Press).
37 Elena Aronova: Popper and Lamarckism. Biological Theory 2 (1) 2007, 37 – 51) Avital, Eytan., Jablonka, Eva :Animal Traditions: Behavioral Inheritance in Evolution. Cambridge University Press 2000.
West-Eberhard Mary Jane :Developmental Plasticity and Evolution. Oxford University Press. 2003.
West-Eberhard, Mary Jane: Dancing with DNA and flirting with the Ghost of Lamarck. Biology and Philosophy 22 (2007) 439 – 451.
Richerson, Peter. J., Robert Boyd: Not by genes alone. How culture transformed human evolution. University of Chicago Press 2005 Günter Wächtershäuser: On the Chemistry and Evolution of Pioneer Organism. Chemistry and Biodiversity Vol 4 (2007) 584 – 602.
Günter Wächtershäuser: Before enzymes and templates: Theory of surface metabolism. Microbiol. Rev. 52 (1988) 452 – 484.
Günter Wächtershäuser: Pyrite formation, the first energy source for life: a hypothesis. Syst. Appl. Microbiol. 10 (1988) 207 – 210.
Günter Wächtershäuser: Evolution of the first metabolic cycle. Proc. Natn. Acad. Sci. U.S.A. 87 (1990) 200 – 2004.
Günter Wächtershäuser: Ground works for an evolutionary biochemistry: the iron-sulfur world. Prog. Biophys. Mol. Biol. 58 (1992), 85 – 201.
Günter Wächtershäuser: The cradle chemistry of life. Pure Appl. Chem. 65 (1993) 1343 – 1348.
Günter Wächtershäuser: Life in a ligand sphere. Proc. Natn. Acad. Sci. U.S.A. 91 (1994) 4283 – 4287.
39 Günter Wächtershäuser: On the Chemistry and Evolution of Pioneer Organism. Chemistry and Biodiversity Vol 4 (2007) 584 – 602.
40 Leslie E. Orgel: The Implausibility of Metabolic Cycles on the Prebiotic earth. PLOS Biology Vol.6 (1) January 2008, p. 5 – 13.

41 for instance Nicholas H. Barton et al.: Evolution. Cold Spring Harbor Laboratory Press, 2007.
42 David Miller: Sir Karl Popper. Biogr. Mems Fell. R. Soc. Lond. 43, 367 – 409 (1997).
43 Eva Jablonka, Lamb Marion: Evolution in Four Dimensions. Genetic, Epigenetic, Behavioral, and Symbolic Variation in the History of Life. A Bradford Book, MIT Press 2005; for a review see [44].
44 West-Eberhard, Mary Jane: Dancing with DNA and flirting with the Ghost of Lamarck. Biology and Philosophy 22 (2007) 439 – 451.
45 West-Eberhard Mary Jane :Developmental Plasticity and Evolution. Oxford University Press. 2003; for a review see [47].
46 Eva Jablonka: Genes as followers in evolution – a post-synthesis synthesis ? Biology and Philosophy 1- 12, 2004.
47 Eytan Avital and Eva Jablonka: Animal Traditions: Behavioral Inheritance in Evolution. Cambridge University Press 2000.
48 Bruce H. Weber, and D.J. Depew Edt.: Evolution and Learning. The Baldwin Effect Reconsidered. A Bradford Book, MIT Press, 2003.
49 Richerson, Peter. J., Robert Boyd: Not by genes alone. How culture transformed human evolution. University of Chicago Press 2005.
50 John Odling-Smee,., K.N.Lalande and M.W.Feldman: Niche construction: The Neglected Process in Evolution. Princeton University Press, 2003.

Annex

Notes on the publication history of Karl Poppers ideas on evolutionary theory.

1930 – 1933   Work on the manuscript of *"Die beiden Grundprobleme der Erkenntnistheorie"*. Starting from the exploratory movements of unicellular organism Popper gives a first sketch of his evolutionary theory of the growth of Knowledge. Parts of this manuscript have been published in 1994.

1935   Draft on a lecture on "Das Elend des Historizismus"

1936   Lectures on "Das Elend des Historizismus" in Brussels and London.

1944, 1945   Divided into three parts the *"The poverty of historicism"* is published in the Journal *Economia*.

1954   Italian publication of *"The poverty of historicism"* in book form. (*Miseria della Storicismo"*)

1956   French publication of *"The poverty of historicism"* in book form (*"Misere de l´Historicime"*)

1957 First English publication of *"The poverty of historicism"* in book form

1961 ***Evolution and the Tree of Knowledge***
Herbert Spencer Lecture, delivered in Oxford on 30 October 1961. The manuscript was deposited on the same day in the Bodleian library. Peter Medawar's criticism led Popper to delay the publication until 1972 when the text was included as chapter 7 in "Objective Knowledge" in an essentially unchanged form, but with addition added in 1971. Later additions also included two additional literature references added in 1974.

1965 ***Of Clouds and Clocks***
Second Arthur Holly Compton Memorial lecture, delivered at Washington University on 21 April 1965. Published as chapter 6 of "Objective Knowledge" with two literature references added in 1974.

1969 ***Knowledge and the Body Mind Problem***
A series of six lectures Popper delivered in spring 1969 as the Kennan Lectures at the Emory University. A transcript of the tape recordings had been prepared in the early seventies and Popper intermittently worked on them to prepare them for publication until 1968 when a preliminary version of the text was sold to the Hover Institution on War, Revolution and Peace and deposited in the Karl Popper Archives at Stanford University. In 1992 M. A. Noturno – in collaboration with Popper – started work on a final revision of the manuscript which was supplemented by transcripts of the discussions and – after being authorized by a short introductory note by Popper – published as *Knowledge and the Body Mind Problem* in 1994.

1972 ***Objective Knowledge: An Evolutionary Approach***
A collection of papers and lectures which contains as chapter 6 "Of clouds and clocks" (the Second Arthur Holy Compton Lecture delivered on 21 April 1965) and as chapter 7 a revised form "Evolution and the Tree of Knowledge" (the Herbert Spencer Lecture delivered on 30 October 1961, slightly updated and with an addendum added in 1971).

1973 *The Rationality of Scientific Revolutions*
Popper's contribution to the six "Herbert Spencer Lectures", a series of lectures given at the Linacre College in Oxford in 1973. Published in 1975 in "Problems of Scientific Revolutions"

1975 *The Philosophy of Karl Popper*
Two volumes on Karl Poppers philosophy published in The Library of living Philosophers, edited by P.A. Schilpp. Volume I containing the Autobiography of Karl Popper with chapter 37 on *"Darwinism as a Metaphysical Research Programme"* and Volume 2 containing **Poppers reply to his critics**, especially chapter 23 with his reply to Donald T. Campbell.

1977 *Natural Selection and the Emergence of Mind*
1. Darwin Lecture delivered on 8 November 1977 at the Darwin College in Cambridge. After a first publication in 1978 in Dialectica Popper added an addendum in 1985 and contributed the revised form to a collection of essays on *Evolutionary Epistemology, Rationality, and the Sociology of Knowledge* published in 1987.

1977 *The Self and its Brain*
The first part of this book is written by Popper, the second part by John Eccles. The third part consists in a transcript of discussions between the two authors.

1983 *Die Zukunft ist offen – Ein Kamingespräch zwischen Konrad Lorenz und Karl Popper.*
Transcript of a discussion between Popper and Lorenz held on 21 February 1983 in Konrad Lorenz home in Altenberg.

Symposium aus dem Anlass des 80. Geburtstages von Karl Popper
Transcript of the symposium held in Vienna 24. – 26 May 1983 including an epilogue written by Popper in 1984.

1986 *Die erkenntnistheoretische Position der Evolutionären Erkenntnistheorie*
Lecture delivered at the Symposium on *Evolutionäre Erkenntnistheorie* which was held in Vienna (18. – 20. April 1986) and published in 1987 in the Symposium volume

Die evolutionäre Erkenntnistheorie and in 1994 in *Alles Leben ist Problemlösen*.
Eine Weiterentwicklung der Darwinschen Theorie
Lecture delivered at the Gesellschaft der Ärzte in Wien on 14 March 1986 Transcript not published
Eine Weiterentwicklung der Darwinschen Theorie. Discussion of Poppers Lecture from 14 March 1986
Discussion of Poppers lecture held at the Gesellschaft der Ärzte Wien on 28 May 1986
A New Interpretation of Darwinism
First Medawar Lecture held on 12 June 1986 in the Royal Society London. (Not published).

1988   ***A World of Propensities: Two new Views of Causality***
Lecture delivered at the World Congress of Philosophy in Brighten on 24 August 1988. A revised and enlarged version was published in 1990 as a chapter of *A World of Propensities*.

1989   **Towards an Evolutionary Theory of Knowledge**
Lecture given for the Alumni of the London School of Economics on 9 June 1989. In enlarged form published 1990 in *A world of Propensities*.

1990   **A World of Propensities**
The book contains enlarged versions of *A World of Propensities: Two new Views of Causality* and *Towards an Evolutionary Theory of Knowledge*

1994   **Knowledge and the Body Mind Problem**
Revised and authorized version of the Kennan Lectures Popper delivered at Emory University in 1969.

Popper's Theory of Objective Knowledge and its Relevance to Modern Knowledge Society

Gerhard Budin

Karl Popper's vision of an Open Society and his theory of the growth of scientific knowledge as well as his World 3 model of knowledge are the points of departure for this paper.

On the one hand, science is producing more new knowledge than ever before, on the other hand there are more and more constraints on this knowledge production: the legal protection of intellectual property rights and the enforcement of strict copyright rules, the ever growing economic pressure of the publishing industry for 'selling' scientific knowledge in the form of high-tech and knowledge intensive products

The current buzzword of the 'knowledge society' is a concept that is very much oriented towards efforts of digitising knowledge production by using modern knowledge engineering techniques. In large organisations (corporate business environments as well as public institutions), the concept of knowledge management offers both, a positive and a negative potential: on the one hand, people feel threatened by current knowledge management efforts where managers seemingly try to disappropriate human (expert) knowledge from employees in order to collect and formalise that knowledge in central knowledge repositories. On the other hand, knowledge management provides a powerful method for identifying the constraints on creating and using knowledge, as well as for finding innovative ways and strategies of how to preserve or even re-inforce the central ethical role scientists should actively play in the so-called knowledge society.

The overall goal is to make sure that this knowledge society will eventually be an Open Society in Popper' sense.

1 The theory of objective knowledge, Popper's world 3

This theory has a long history, both in the histories of science and of philosophy, and in Popper's intellectual development. Popper mentions Plato as the first major representative of a kind of objectivist theory concerning concepts and ideas existing independently of man, i.e. independently of cognitive processes. After a long history and fundamentally different versions, Popper arrives, at long last, in 1972 at a relatively mature theory of objective knowledge, that has its roots in his early works on thought psychology in the 1920s, and that he continuously comes back to in later years. Another landmark in his intellectual history is 1963 with Conjectures and Refutations, and a series of lectures in the 1950s and 1960s and early 1970s that constitute the 1972 collation.

Popper's three worlds model is essentially interactionistic: the distinction of world 1 of physical objects and processes from a world 2 of cognitive processes and from a world 3 of the content of thoughts, i.e. theories, problems, the contents of books, the design of human artefacts, etc. can best be understood when considering the interaction of any of these worlds with any of the two others: world 3 is a product of world 2, world 1 is a pre-requisite but also a result of world 2 and its interaction with world 3, the interaction between worlds 1 and 3 is only possible through world 2, etc.

The clear separation of worlds 2 and 3 together with some specification of how they interact and constitute each other is a major achievement in the history of science and epistemology, since it overcomes psychologism without falling into the trap of the other extreme, i.e. antipsychologism. It is interesting to note that several recent theories or practice domains are prone to fall prey to either of the two extremes: e.g. knowledge management, that I will come back to in a minute, is essentially psychologistic, because knowledge is usually defined and limited there following Michael Polanyi's paradigm of tacit, personal knowledge only, although some approaches at least openly admit that there is a contradiction because they also talk about organisational knowledge, intellectual capital of a company, etc. The same problem is true in cognitivistic versions of philosophy of science that reduce science to the individual cognitive processes of scientists, as well as cognitivistic approaches to knowledge engineering.

A purpose of this paper, therefore, is to remind ourselves in these important and future-oriented domains that Karl Popper's contribution of a theory of objective knowledge is a necessary and useful complementary element in novel approaches in knowledge management and in knowledge engineering, as well as for the future of philosophy of science.

But let me come back to Popper's world 3 and its objective knowledge. Various paraphrases are formulated by Popper: knowledge without a knowing subject, etc.

In different chapters of the 1972 book and in different papers and previous books, he explicitly mentions several precursors of his theory he is building upon: in particular Frege, 1892 (the objective content of thoughts), before that Bolzano 1837, but also Husserl and Gomperz and Meinong (theory of objects), so he was building on an objectivistic tradition – but also in line with his earlier work on thought psychology, and in line with Karl Bühler, Otto Selz, Külpe, etc. in this tradition of thought psychology

But he also cites general language usage by referring to the Oxford English Dictionary that also differentiates between knowledge as a state of being informed, etc. and knowledge as a science, as art, etc.

He also refers to a contemporary thinker with whom he was in line: Hayek – as Brian Caldwell showed in a very interesting paper in July 2002, the mutual influence between Hayek and Popper was not so big, but their lines of thinking were highly compatible.

The argumentative function he adds to Bühler's linguistic model is of high importance in this context: objective knowledge is always the result of an argumentation process, it is public knowledge, is knowledge represented by language or any other semiotic means. Popper points out that language itself is part of world 3, but at the same time other aspects of language are part of world 1 and world 2. Linguistic argumentation has thus a crucial role not only in science, but society at large.

Other important aspects of this theory of objective knowledge are its evolutionary character and its hypothetical character. Both aspects are essentially inseparable: there is no final knowledge, we can never be absolutely sure that what we know is true or that a certain theory is true (again interaction worlds 2 and 3), thus the inherently hypothetical nature of all knowledge, including scientific knowledge, therefore scientific knowledge always develops further. Popper's famous schema of the growth of scientific knowledge by error elimination and the establishment of a new hypothesis and new problems to be solved in the next loop is a simple formalisation of these processes. This dynamics can easily be called evolutionary, in analogy to Darwin's classical evolutionary theory, an obvious analogy that led to evolutionary epistemology (Campbell 1974), with 2 programmes (Wuketits 1999): the evolution of cognition, the evolution of science and scientific knowledge (Lorenz – Popper, et al.)

Other aspects of Popper's methodology of science are relevant as well: testability, refutability, fallibilism, falsifiability, but they are not treated in this context here.

2 What is the relevance of this theory to the knowledge society?

First we have to ask what the buzzword of knowledge society means. A convergence process of long developments of several industrial revolutions (digitisation, automation, computers, Internet, etc.) leading to (but not being the single and only cause of) fundamental changes in society, incl. work relations, professions, divisions of labour, type of work, the rise of service industry, new economy, etc., new social forms of living, etc. The older buzzword of the information society is still around und pervasively used.

In 1998 Helmut Spinner provided a systematic model of a knowledge-oriented architecture of the information society with a detailed typology of knowledge activities, in addition to existing or emerging information policies in our countries, we also need explicit knowledge policies (e.g. Finland), focusing on information literacy and knowledge literacy.

The mere focus on ICT (Information and Communication Technology) is obviously wrong, information literacy is about how to find quality information, how to select, evaluate information on the web, i.e. how to *make sense* of technology.

On the technical level of these developments, we encounter many more buzzwords: artificial intelligence, intelligent agents, ontology engineering, language engineering, knowledge engineering, reasoning, Internet, web, telerobotics, virtual reality, computer simulation, etc. The impact of these fast developments on the human mind, on the development of epistemology still has to be studied in detail. For an interesting debate on telepistemology, as defined by Goldberg (2000) as the study of knowledge at a distance, see Levy 1994 who also talks about collective intelligence, cosmopedia (Levy 1994), while Rheingold and Gibson introduced concepts such as virtual communities, cyberscpace. The lines between reality and imagination have never been as blurred as today when we think of new "realities" such as "Augmented Reality" that leads to "augmented knowledge".

On a more down-to-earth level we do use Collaboratories (the term consisting of "collaborative" denoting the basic working principle, and "laboratory", nowadays usually in the form of web-based distributed knowledge systems. Thinking about Popper's theory of objective knowledge, the immediate and burning question arises: which criteria should we establish and use to differentiate this objective knowledge residing in such systems from mere data collections, from information? The property of "objectivity" that knowledge has in the Popperian concept seems to be based on the fact that knowledge is codified in books etc. and therefore has become independent of the creator, i.e. from the brain of the creator, so it has shifted from a subjective mind to an objective level of verifiable re-usable and processable information structures that make sense to a whole group of people (we have moved from world 2 to world 3, from the subjective intra-mind level to the intersubjective level of inter-mind communication). So when an online community of people jointly uses such a collaboratory with a knowledge repository that people feed into on a regular basis, the criteria for objective knowledge seems to be met.

In the area of computational philosophy of science, Paul Thagard has proposed a method of computational reconstruction of the genesis of theories (a conceptual approach to modelling assertions and argumentation structures). Knowledge engineering (John Sowa 2000) has led to a more refined knowledge typology (declarative, procedural, etc.), and many true knowledge bases have emerged. We can claim that objective knowledge in Popper's sense is residing in such systems, provided that before a number of steps have taken place before: data is interpreted and aggregated in meaningful ways -> information is emerging as a result -> on the basis of information, knowledge is emerging in personal knowledge acquisition processes, and in groups (argumentation, critical aspect), cognitive processes (world 2) took place before knowledge is codified in a book and thereby becomes objective knowledge in world 3 that has a real content. Now we even differentiate content from knowledge and knowledge management from content management: content is objective knowledge packaged and processed to become a specific product for a specific audience, in a specific multimedia presentation form.

I now return to knowledge management: I already described the fundamental contradiction of the discussion on knowledge in KM (Communication Management) – interaction between worlds 2 and 3 is again crucial – both is concerned, to be differentiated in order to make KM more effective!

The following key processes in Knowledge management can be mapped to Popperian worlds 2 and 3 in the following way:

Knowledge	Process	"Worlds" involved
	Identification	2 (who knows what), 3 (data mining, patent search, search for codified K etc.

Creation	2 (cognitive creation by each researcher etc., also in groups), interaction with 3 e.g. when writing (epistemic effects!)
Storage, Preservation	2 (individual memory), 3 (in books, databases or knowledge repositories, etc.
Communication	3 (presentation, transformation, using semiotic means, argumentation, criticism)
Dissemination	3 (communication, transfer – teaching learning, electronic distribution, providing Electronic access
Use	2, 3

Knowledge Sharing has become one of the key concepts in the field of knowledge management.

Coming back to the popularity of Polanyi in KM communities: Sheldon Richmond has proposed to combine Popper and Polanyi in order to overcome the limitations or biases of both – they are complementary (Polanyi's focus on tacit personal knowledge, cognitive aspects (world 2), Popper's focus on world 3 (but his model is not that one-sided) and objective knowledge, so this proposal seems to be make sense.

3 The concept of Open Society and the theory of knowledge

There are parallels between the two concepts: knowledge is never perfect and sure, the society is never perfect always needs active work to be improved. Imperfect societies have an infinite potential for improvement – the same is true for knowledge.

For an open society to work properly, it is essential to have functioning information and knowledge policies, regulating the access to information and to knowledge and the possibilities for citizens to actively participate in what we call information society or knowledge society.

Only knowledgeable citizens are able to participate in an open society. Critical thinking is crucial, founded on a knowledge basis of world 2 knowledge of each participant and world 3 knowledge as – for instance – contained in libraries.

Popper mentions libraries when talking about world 3: In fact these libraries as knowledge repositories par excellence play a crucial role in an open knowledge society.

Robinson and Bawden (2001) list 7 principles concerning the role of libraries and librarians in an open society (incl. Critical thinking)

- the importance of provision of access to a wide variety of sources without 'negative' restriction or censorship
- the need for provision of 'positive' guidance on sources, based on open and objective criteria
- a recognition that a 'free flow of information' though essential, is not sufficient
- a recognition that provision of factual information, while valuable, is not enough
- a need for specific concern for the effect of new information and communication technologies, and of the Internet in particular
- the importance of the promotion of critical thinking and digital literacy, both among the library profession and among our patrons
- a need for a more explicit consideration of the ethical values of libraries and librarians than has been the case

In the 1930s and 1940s Hayek and Popper dealt with very similar topics. In 1937 and 1945 Hayek published two articles (one of them is "The Use of Knowledge in Society") that have not lost any of their importance for contemporary society, in fact they became, together with Vannevar Bush's "As we may think" (also 1945), the foundational texts for knowledge management and for the modern information economy, (and in the case of Bush also a forefather of hypertext and of information engineering)

In the Open Society, Popper wrote about the sources of knowledge – every source of knowledge (without authority) is allowed, but no source is immune from criticism…not the source is important but the content, to be critically evaluated

Thus it is not the role of the librarian to deny access to such (maybe dubious) sources , but rather to guide users of how to deal with such sources, and how to critically evaluate their content. Therefore it is essential to have a transparent policy in libraries and information services of which sources are selected and on which grounds/criteria (budget, copyright, etc.)

Complementary to that, there is an increasing role of meta-data systems, providing an overview of all sources that are in theory available, but (out of necessity of lack of space and budget) not available in any location at any time at no cost.

Public information must be provided in comprehensible form! Public libraries have an important role in local communities (social function as a communication space), a learning centre, provoking reflexive processes, critical thinking, thought provoking, etc. Information and Communication Technologies are obviously helping them to perform this function and role much more efficiently than before.

4 Digital libraries

The term "digital libraries" refers to a rather technical movement focusing on syntactic encoding of information collections, but again it is crucial to add the content dimension and the question of use, free access, etc. Again we are confronted in this context with the paradox of the Internet: a lot of information is available for free, but new hurdles and information barriers are created in the same medium: the lack of knowledge organisation, the problem of finding relevant, high quality information. This is the reason why special services by information specialists are required to help the public to find their way in this information maze. Concepts such as "Digital literacy", "information literacy" have become so popular today.

The American Library Association defined six components of information literacy (in Robinson/Bawden 2001):
- recognising a need for information
- identifying what information would address a particular problem
- finding the needed information
- evaluating the information found
- organising the information
- using the information effectively in addressing the specific problem

plus hypertextual navigation and knowledge assembly for digital literacy, plus critical thinking – asking informed questions, posing problems in various ways before attempting to solve them, examining assumptions, evaluating source of information, assessing the quality of one's own thinking and problem-solving, (Gilster 1997, Bawden 2001)

Robinson and Bawden cite the New Zealand Library Association as early as 1952 (p. 122f): "the library can be the most valuable instrument of democracy and good citizenship. Where no library exists, books written by zealots and propagandists, and newspapers which tend to be sensational, can be potent weapons of subversion. But a good library service providing material in open, well-balanced, many-sided collections can help to make democracy sane, informed, stable and real". It is quite interesting to read this visionary statement that is now 56 years old but that did not loose any of its importance for today.

Education is closely related to libraries as knowledge repositories: A well-known cognitive scientist, Carl Bereiter, investigated the role of education in the knowledge society of the 21st century. What are the skills that have to be acquired to become a full citizen of the knowledge society and how should these skills be acquired?

These skills coincide with those that are currently required in business and industry from young managers. Knowledge is a third factor in addition to capital and labour and metaphorically called intellectual capital; skills as imagination, creativity, teamwork, communication skills, information-finding skills, problem-solving abilities, technological literacy, readiness to learn, are needed today.

5 "Enculturation into World 3"

Carl Bereiter talks about a sort of knowledge ability, differentiating 2 kinds of knowledge (worlds 2 and 3): "knowledge is something that people acquire and that becomes a part of them (world 2, learning), second, knowledge is something they work with and that in some sense takes on a life of its own (world 3)"

Learning is taking place in world 2, while knowledge-building in happening in world 3 (cooperative, explicit, etc.): "World 3 is a workspace where knowledge objects are in various stages of development. Some are finished to the extent that no one bothers to tinker with them anymore. Others are under current development and are the subjects of research, criticism, controversy, repair operations, and novel conjecture...." (Bereiter)

He cites Popper from the 1972 book: "I suggest that one day we will have to revolutionize psychology by looking at the human mind as an organ for interacting with the objects in the third world; for understanding them, contributing to them, participating in them; and for bringing them to bear on the first world."

This is not only a work programme for schools to prepare children for the knowledge society and to provide digital literacy, but also a vision for usability engineering and human computer interaction (HCI) research and practice.

A new role for educational institutions is shaping up: not only in world 2, but also in world 3, knowledge production becomes a task. Educational institutions can benefit from their collaborative workspaces and dynamic social configurations for promoting the cooperation between companies and educational institutions to support each other in learning and knowledge production. Increasingly, universities and also schools have to be become knowledge building organisations themselves, opening up to other spheres of society and thereby fulfilling the basic functions they are needed for in a much more efficient way.

6 Outlook

Christine Borgman's vision of a global information infrastructure still requires a lot of work (the technical level is the smallest problem), but rather copyright issues and other information barriers, semantic interoperability of distributed information resources, and even more importantly, social issues, the question of knowledge literacy, and ethical questions have to be addressed, discussed, and hopefully solved.

I tried to show that Karl Popper's theory of knowledge is not outdated and in fact is crucial for the future of global society at large. Of course much remains to be discussed and many details to be clarified in this respect.

7 Literature

Bawden, David. Information and digital literacy's; a review of concepts. Journal of Documentation, 57 (2), 218-259, 2001

Bereiter, Carl. Education in a Knowledge Society, 2001

Bolzano, Bernhard. Wissenschaftslehre 1837

Borgman, Christine. From Gutenberg to the Global Information Infrastructure. Access to Information in the Networked World. MIT Press, 2000

Bush, Vannevar. As we may think. Atlantic Monthly, 1945

Frege, Gottlob. Über Sinn und Bedeutung. Zeitschrift für Philosophie und philosophische Kritik, 100, 1892, 25-50

Gilster, Paul. Digital Literacy. New York: Wiley, 1997

Goldberg, Ken. Telepistemology. In Goldberg (ed.). The Robot in the Garden. Telerobotics and Telepistemology in the Age of the Internet. MIT Press, 2000

Hayek, Friedrich von. The Use of Knowledge in Society. 1945

Levy, Paul. Cosmopedie. Paris, 1994

New Zealand Library Association. National Library Service Annual Report, New Zealand Libraries, 1952

Polanyi, Michael. Personal Knowledge, 1958

Popper, Karl. Conjectures and Refutations. The Growth of Scientific Knowledge. London: Routledge, 1963

Popper, Karl. Objective Knowledge. An Evolutionary Approach. Oxford: Clarendon Press, 1972

Richmond, Sheldon. The Two Cultures Problem. 20th World Congress of Philosophy, 1998

Robinson Lyn/ Bawden David. Libraries, information and knowledge in open societies. Budapest/London 2001

Spinner, Helmut. Die Architektur der Informationsgesellschaft. Entwurf eines wissensorientierten Gesamtkonzepts. Bodenheim: Philo, 1998

Thagard, Paul. Computational Philosophy of Science. Cambridge, Mass: MIT Press, 1988

Veltman, Kim. Understanding New Media: Augmented Knowledge and Culture, 2004

Contributors

Bryan Magee: Philosopher, Writer and Broadcaster; Fellow of Wolfson College, Oxford, former MP, taught philosophy as lecturer or visiting fellow at Yale, Harvard, Oxford and Cambridge and Sidney.

Troels Eggers Hansen: Library of University Roskilde. Editor of Poppers "Frühe Schriften" and "Die beiden Grundprobleme der Erkenntnistheorie".

Hubert Kiesewetter: former Professor of Economic and Social History at the University Eichstätt. Editor of German editions of "Das Elend des Historizismus" und die "Die offene Gesellschaft und ihre Feinde".

Erich Kadlec: Chairman of the Karl Popper Institute, wrote "Praktische Philosophie – heute: Mit Karl Popper zur Grundlegung einer Universalmoral" 2007 and "Realistische Ethik" 1976.

Peter Markl: Professor for Analytical Chemistry and lecturer in the methodology of science at Vienna university. Member of the Konrad Lorenz Institute for Evolution and Cognition Research and the scientific advisory board of the European Forum Alpbach. Former Member of the International Pugwash Council, Staatspreis für journalistische Leitungen im Dienst von Wissenschaft und Forschung.

Gerhard Budin: Dean, Centre of Translation – Science, Vienna University wrote "Knowledge Organisation for a Global Learning Society".

Leviathan Between the Wars

Hobbes' Impact on Early Twentieth Century Political Philosophy
Edited by Luc Foisneau, Jean-Christophe Merle and Tom Sorell

Frankfurt am Main, Berlin, Bern, Bruxelles, New York, Oxford, Wien, 2005.
167 pp.
Rechtsphilosophische Hefte. Editor in charge: Ulrich Steinvorth. Vol. XI
ISBN 978-3-631-51239-5 · pb. € 33.20*

The symbol of the Leviathan came to the forefront in political theory, as the structure and the ideological justification of the state underwent radical change in at least three European countries from the early 1920s to the 1940s. Thus, the terrifying image of Leviathan has sometimes given rise to a surprising historiography of twentieth-century totalitarian states, tracing them back to the origins of modern political thought, as if there were a direct line of descent from Hobbes to Mussolini, Hitler and Stalin, or, worse still, as if Hobbes's *Leviathan* (1651) were an exact anticipation of twentieth-century political catastrophes. The differing interpretations of Hobbes proposed by Strauss, Tönnies, Schmitt, Vialatoux, Capitant, Pareto, Collingwood, and Oakeshott, are here interpreted in the perspective of the interwar transformation of Europe. The contributors, who are German, British and French political philosophers, analyse the conditions which have made possible conflicting readings of Hobbes's political philosophy, and explain why they sometimes don't do justice to *Leviathan*.

Contents: Hobbes · *Leviathan* · Political Philosophy · Europe Between the Wars · Schmitt · Strauss · Oakeshott · Capitant

Frankfurt am Main · Berlin · Bern · Bruxelles · New York · Oxford · Wien
Distribution: Verlag Peter Lang AG
Moosstr. 1, CH-2542 Pieterlen
Telefax 00 41 (0) 32/376 17 27

*The €-price includes German tax rate
Prices are subject to change without notice
Homepage http://www.peterlang.de